W9-CMG-407

THE PILGRIMS IN THEIR THREE HOMES

ENGLAND, HOLLAND, AMERICA

BY

WILLIAM ELLIOT GRIFFIS

REVISED EDITION

Deus fecit

BOSTON AND NEW YORK
HOUGHTON MIFFLIN COMPANY
The Riverside Press Cambridge

IN GRATEFUL MEMORY

OF

MY ENGLISH ANCESTORS

OF NOTTINGHAM AND DEVON

THE SHIRES MOST CLOSELY CONNECTED WITH

PILGRIM HISTORY

AND IN HEARTY ADMIRATION OF THE

MIGHTY ENGLAND WHICH IS

AND THE NOBLER ENGLAND

THAT IS YET TO BE

PREFACE TO THE NEW EDITION

On the 24th of February, 1890, the Boston Congregational Club passed the following resolution: —

Whereas, Remembering the hospitality of the free republic of Holland, so generously bestowed upon the Pilgrims, who, after twelve years' residence in Amsterdam and Leyden, sailed from Delfshaven on a voyage which was completed at Plymouth Rock, it is fitting that we, members of Congregational Clubs throughout the United States, should unite in grateful recognition of Dutch hospitality, and at Delfshaven raise some durable token of our appreciation of both hosts and guests, — calling upon all Americans who honor alike the principles and the founders of the two republics to join in the enterprise. Therefore be it

Resolved, That the Club heartily approves of the erection of such a commemorative monument.

In continuation of a purpose formed by the author, who was a member of the club, to carry out the spirit and provisions of this resolution, he, in addition to his first tour in Holland in 1869, made, between the years 1891 and 1913, eight journeys in Europe in the track of the Pilgrim Fathers. He visited the places of their homes and studied in the archives of England and the Netherlands, mastering the Dutch language sufficiently to be free from taking second-hand opinions.

Having begged the money in America, he superintended the erection, dedication and unveiling of bronze tablets at Middelburg, Amsterdam and Delfshaven. These were designed, from data furnished by himself, by Mr. Charles R. Lamb of the firm of J. & R. Lamb Co., of New York. Three of the ten bronze tablets erected by him in Holland recall the life and work of the founders of Christian democracy as expressed in the Congregational faith and order, of which the Pilgrims were true exemplars.

Yet the first founders of Massachusetts were not merely representatives of church polity. They were men and women of beautiful life and of attractive character. If they had the infirmities and limitations of other mortals, they also showed those touches of nature which make the whole world kin. I have tried to depict them amidst the hopes and fears, the joys and sorrows, of their daily environment in three lands.

In the edition of 1898, I uttered the hope, "May passing time but brighten, and added truth but illuminate, the inspiring Pilgrim story."

The additional chapter XXIV, entitled "Transfiguration," in this new edition of 1914, shows how rich has been the fulfillment. So far from receding into dimness, the increasing lustre of the Pilgrim story is rather like that of the electric arc, after the oil lamp and candle. The added matter shows how grandly three nations have united to honor the founders of New England. Perhaps more than any other single element in history, the Pilgrim story has, in recent years, furnished a fresh and abiding bond of union between the two greatest of the English-speaking nations.

W. E. G.

ITHACA, N. Y., *May* 7, 1914.

CONTENTS

THE

PILGRIMS IN THEIR THREE HOMES

CHAPTER I

INTRODUCTION AND COMPARISON

All English-speaking people ought to know the difference between the Pilgrims and the Puritans. The Pilgrims separated Church and State. They believed in the right and power of Christian people to govern themselves, and they believed this when, even in England, it was dangerous to breathe such an idea. They were hunted out of their home-land into the Dutch republic, where conscience was free. Thence they crossed the stormy ocean, and began on American soil the experiment of self-government.

To-day their descendants, direct and collateral, may number a million. They are found in all the States of the Union, and among Christians of every name. By them the heroic Pilgrim ancestors have been transfigured, their story has been embalmed in art and poetry, and kept alive in monuments and in celebrations. Descent from a

Pilgrim father or mother is like a patent of nobility. New England societies, Congregational clubs and churches of many names, from Sandy Hook to the Golden Gate, from the fresh-water ocean to the hot salt gulf, annually recount their merits, and retell the old story. In all lands where the English tongue is sweet to the ear, their name is honored. Whittier, in order to make known the German Pastorius, who first in the region of the United States protested against slavery, has to call him "The Pennsylvania Pilgrim."

Tens of thousands of tourists each year visit the old historic spots at Plymouth. The boulder from the far north, which in history was only a threshold, has become in rhetoric mountain-large, though as keepsake and paper-weight as small as a scarab. By Longfellow the poet, Hawthorne the romancer, Boughton the painter, historiographers by the score, a library of books concerning them, great pictures in the national Capitol rotunda at Washington, and vignettes on the national bank-notes, the Pilgrims are well advertised. A mighty shaft on Plymouth heights, with its pedestal cuirassed with bas-reliefs, surmounted and flanked with sculptures, and another of lesser proportions at Provincetown overlook the sands of their third home. Bronze tablets at Scrooby, Leyden, Provincetown, and the two Plymouths serve to keep bright their memory. Relics of stone, on which their feet may have trodden, are built into the façades and walls of great churches. The two great English-speaking people thrill when the miscalled "Log of the Mayflower" — the book of Genesis in the history of Massachusetts — recrosses the ocean. Their fame has gone throughout the world, and their glorious testimony to the ends of the earth.

Their story is worth telling without fear or favor, in simple style for young people, as I shall try to tell it.

Strange to say, their place of origin was not known to living men until half a century ago. Not only during their own lives, but long after they had passed away, the Pilgrims, now immortal in American history and in the story of human progress, were like the "poor wayfaring man of grief," so far as their king or country cared. When they left England, nobody recked whither they went. In Holland few inquired whence they came. James Stuart, their "dread sovereign," was only sorry that he could not lay violent hands on them while in their Dutch asylum. They were plucked, like fowls for the spit, by the Merchant Adventurers. Besides utterly neglecting Dutch history, few Americans, except John Adams, took the trouble to visit their old home in Leyden. Until near the year 1850, their descendants, and our own and the English nation, could not place the Pilgrims' cradle-land.

This was finally discovered to be just where

William Bradford, their historian, who wrote the first book of American history, said it was. Bradford's work, dubbed by the English newspapers "The Log of the Mayflower," but by the author entitled the "History of Plimouth Plantation," is the written volume which our English friends in 1897 restored to us. It was the property of the Old South Church of Boston, from whose library it had been taken in Revolutionary days. Our first ambassador to Great Britain, Thomas Francis Bayard, brought it across the sea, and on Wednesday, the twenty-seventh of May, 1897, it was delivered to the State of Massachusetts, in the archives of which it now rests.

Bradford, writing between the years 1640 and 1650, says that these people of three homes and two continents were originally "of several towns and villages, some in Nottinghamshire, some in Lincolnshire, and some in Yorkshire, where they bordered nearest together." Yet although this statement was copied by Prince in his annals, and though Cotton Mather, in a sketch of Bradford's life, writes that he was born at A*n*sterfield, there was a riddle which for over two centuries stood like a sphinx in American literature. The puzzle was not solved till an American and an Englishman put their heads together, and penetrated the mystery.

That little misprinted letter *n* was as the symbol *x* in algebra, — an unknown quantity which baffled those who tried to solve the problem. No such place could be found in all England, ancient or modern. Instead of an *n* it ought to have been a *u*. When Mr. James Savage, of Massachusetts, the genealogist, in 1842 visited the Rev. John Hunter, a native and an historian of Yorkshire, this English gentleman discovered Austerfield and the baptismal record of William Bradford. In 1849, in a little book, he told what he had found out about the "Founders of New Plymmouth."

Even before this, however, the Leyden professor, N. C. Kist, and the Mennonite scholar, Dr. J. G. D. Scheffer, of Amsterdam, who had read the Dutch records of two cities, discovered much of delightful interest; for Holland is rich in Pilgrim memories. After these have come a host of wise men from both west and east of the Atlantic, who have searched diligently to find where the young Pilgrim republic was born. Every year the twilight becomes more like day and mysteries vanish. The hidden church now shines forth. The story is luminous and nearly complete. New links of interest bind us as Americans to the mother-country of England and the fatherland of Holland. "History is a resurrection."

To understand why these North Country folk left "Merrie England," we must ride backward on the winged wheel of imagination to the opening of the sixteenth century. Three hundred years ago everything, except human nature and the ocean and sky, was quite different from what we see in our time. Dress and food, manners and customs, politics and religion, houses and the way of living, farming and crops, the relations of land and water, and the outlook of people on the great world and the countries beyond, were not as now. Think of living, even in cities, where there were no newspapers, railways, telegraphs, telephones, photographs, matches, fire engines, water pipes, tinware, china dishes, tea or coffee. Fancy villages where brick houses and iron ploughs, underclothing and starch, — "the Devil's liquid," as the Puritan Stubbes called it, — were just beginning to come into fashion, and where these novelties from the continent were hardly more than curiosities.

Then paved roads, fenced or hedged fields, post-offices, postage stamps, and letters carried by government for the people were unknown. Then England was a weak and sparsely populated country of about four million people. In large portions of it, and even where is now good farm-land, were great areas of swamp, heath, and forest. Most of the eastern counties consisted of reedy marshes, above which uncounted wild fowl wheeled in the air, while only here and there were patches of ploughed land. Then the seven states of the Dutch republic had only eight hundred thousand inhabitants. All of what is now the United States of America was but a savage wilderness inhabited by possibly a third of a million of Indians, and a few hundred Spaniards in New Mexico and Florida. How strange it must have been to live in those times, and how hard to imagine now how people got along then!

Fortunately for the present writer, this is not so very difficult a thing for him to do. I can hold up a mirror and draw from experience. Even in this nineteenth century, I lived during four years in an island empire much like Great Britain. During one whole year, while in a city of forty thousand people, rich in castle towers, drawbridges, moats, guilds, and things mediæval and feudalistic, I saw no newspaper, milk wagon, telegraph, telephone, railway, horse carriage or wagon, gas lamp, iron or terra cotta water pipe, stationary washstand, or house furnished with water, other than from wells. There were very few of the modern things or ideas. The condition of society, state, and church was like that of sixteenth-century Europe. There were castles and cathedrals, abbots and armed men. All gentlemen wore swords. The land was not owned by those who worked it, but was rented, through many grades of rank, from the sovereign to lords temporal and spiritual. Except the yeomen, or franklins, who were freeholders, the agricultural laborers were not much better than serfs.

The king was hedged about with divinity, and

supposed to get all his power direct from Heaven. When he appeared in public, common folks fell down on their knees. Religion was a matter of the state, governed by the court and the politicians. People who did not agree with the state church were persecuted, thrown into prison, or put to death. Yet, paradoxical as it may seem, these nineteenth-century heretics, or separatists, were not allowed to leave the country. Exactly as in sixteenth-century England, a large part of the best land was owned by the monasteries, which like the monks and nuns were very numerous, a great ecclesiastical corporation controlled human life from the cradle to the grave, and the "tortures of hell were graded according to the money" paid the priests in temple, monastery, or chantry, who had charge of masses. The priests had sharp eyes upon the deathbed of the wealthy. These who would not give or will much property to the religious corporations were pretty sure to be damned.

In this country, in which I dwelt nearly four years, torture was used in the courts, just as in Europe, and even in England, until the reign of William III. In law and science the people were no better off than in religion. Strange and curious superstitions fettered the minds of both learned and unlearned in matters of building, crops, the weather, and household and social life, just as in the old Europe where our pagan and our Christian forefathers lived. Here, also, were witchcraft, sorcery, plague, pestilence, and famine, besides pretty material for legend and fairy tale. Outwardly the different classes of people were marked by their dress. The bishops, as well as the nobles, abbots, and priests, wore peculiar uniforms. Nobles of church or state had many idle followers, retainers, and servants, who were attired in their masters' livery. Parades and shows made fine sights for the people, who were fleeced by these gayly dressed fellows; for king, princes, earls, dukes, marquises, barons, and all degrees of nobility and gentry lived off "the commons," among whom were yeomen, farmers, mechanics, and others little better than slaves. There were craftsmen's guilds and trade monopolies, just as in old Europe. The merchant was socially of small account. The noblemen, priests, and gentlemen made society. The tenant farmer was respected, but was ground down to support those above him. People in each grade of society dressing in a different way, there was a great variety of costume. Matters of clothes and etiquette, splendor and show, old customs and festivities, were of vast importance. There was nothing of what we call underclothing, though there was plenty of silk and gay equipment, but the majority of the people lived very plainly as to dress and food. There were no brick houses. Ploughs and other farm tools were of a very rude sort.

When the reformation came, which has made a new nation of these island dwellers, and the revenues of the monasteries were confiscated, there were insurrections of the rudely armed people led by reactionary and impoverished nobles, gentlemen and priests, wonderfully like the "Pilgrimage of Grace" and the "Uprising in the North," as in old England of the sixteenth century. The description of one country will do for the other.

In a word, this country in which I lived was surprisingly like sixteenth-century England at a thousand points, whether we look at the landscape, which had few or no fences or hedges, but plenty of feudal castles, monasteries, and nunneries, or at the oddly dressed characters going up and down the horse tracks and footpaths, — for there were few roads, in the modern sense of the term. All around were shrines and objects of religion and superstition, with plenty of beggars, lepers, and miserably poor folk. Instead of post-offices, there were, besides inns for meals and beds, relays, where people in government employ could secure horses or burden bearers, exactly as on the great North Road between London and Edinburgh.

Curiously enough also, these times, during which I lived at the capital of a baron, among his retainers and under the shadow of his castle near a monastery, were politically just like the times of Queen Elizabeth. In the matter of social changes, economic progress, the introduction of foreign notions and machines and people to work them, and of the transformation of the whole nation from an agricultural to a commercial and manufacturing people, the country of my sojourn was just like Elizabethan England. A closer union was being formed between the throne and the people. The court peers, landed nobles, and lords spiritual were becoming of less importance. The merchants were rising in social dignity. The old life was everywhere being modified because of foreign ideals, customs, and importations. The simple industries carried on in dwelling-houses were changing to multiplied and varied activities. The weavers, potters, and mechanics, instead of having looms, wheels, and anvils in their own houses, were being assembled into factories. Life from 1870 to 1874 in this island empire, at one end of the earth's greatest land division, appeared, as in a theatre, to be the reproduction on a stage of the life on that island empire at the other end, at a time when the founders of Massachusetts were boys and girls in England. Old Japan illustrated Old England, and New Japan, New England. Race and color of skin and form of religion might be different, but human nature was the same.

Note also two strange coincidences. Just when the Pilgrim fathers and mothers in the Mayflower were leaving their old home-land, which had been shut against them, to open a new world, the ancient empire was expelling the Jesuits, welcoming the Dutch at Déshima, and barring its gates against all other foreigners.

Over two centuries later, in 1848, exactly when Mr. Hunter was discovering the Pilgrims' home and Bradford's baptismal record, the shipwrecked American sailor, Ronald McDonald, from Sag Harbor, New York, became the first teacher of the English language in the sealed empire, and thus the real founder of her new national education. The whaling ship which carried him to Japan was named Plymouth. When the star of Perry's broad pennant was mirrored in the clear waters of Yedo Bay, his oldest ship bore the same name, Plymouth. When Japanese officers asked private sailor and plenipotentiary commodore the supreme source of authority in the United States, both answered "The people."

The Pilgrim faith had but deepened and expanded.

Come then, fellow Americans and speakers of the English tongue, subjects of King Shakespeare and inheritors of the Pilgrim idea of government, and let us visit England at about the latitude, though not in the climate of Labrador, between the fifty-third and fifty-fourth degrees, where Nottinghamshire and Lincolnshire adjoin. We shall stand upon Gringley-on-the-Hill, over which the lad Will Bradford used to walk in going to church at Gainsborough, and from which the view is fine and far. We select him as our typical Pilgrim. His life comprehends the whole of the poetic and heroic period of the Pilgrim story. After him, we name Brewster. For convenience, to avoid circumlocutions and to save space, I shall at once and throughout this book speak of the company led by Brewster, Robinson, and Bradford as "The Pilgrims."

Of my four visits to Scrooby, the home of Brewster, the first was made with a great company. It was in 1891, when to the International Council in London it seemed as if "dear mother England" were calling back her outcast children. Few Englishmen had then visited the place, or knew where it was. On "Bank Holiday" in 1892, desiring a second leisurely sight of the Pilgrim cradle-land, I started from Lincoln. I asked at this station, which is on a great railway and within thirty miles of the village, for a ticket to Scrooby. The agent knew not the name of the place. He compelled me to repronounce and spell the word, but was still incredulous as to the existence of such a station. So I "booked" for Bawtry, and then walked up to Scrooby. The hamlet is now visited annually by scores, perhaps hundreds of Americans. Worksop, the home of my Eyre ancestors, is a few miles to the southwest.

CHAPTER II

AUSTERFIELD AND THE PILGRIM DISTRICT

Many things have changed in our fathers' old home — dear and mighty England — since the flight of the Pilgrims from Scrooby. Even the very memory of their exodus to Holland died out long ago from this region. Yet the landscape is much the same, though that too has changed in respect of surface water, which is far less than then. On all the slope from the central hills of the island toward the North Sea and the Wash, the ground was once very wet and swampy, and much more liable to overflow from the Humber, the Ouse, and the Trent rivers, than it is now. Indeed, the whole line of eastern counties from Essex to York formed a great fen region, full of standing as well as of flowing water, with only here and there hard ground which served as roads, sites for towns, and soil for cultivation. Ely got its name because it was an *eely* place, and the telltale terminations of many places ending in "wick," "beach," "holme," "beck," and "hoe," suggesting low places near or on water, show what they were formerly.

Names ending in "ford" and "bridge," indicating that there had to be some way for getting across the water, are plentiful. For the traveler, there was always "one more river to cross." John Bunyan, in his "Pilgrim's Progress," Defoe, in his "Tour through the Eastern Counties," Jean Ingelow, in her "High Tide on the Coast of Lincolnshire," and Charles Kingsley, in his classic paper on "The Fens," have made wonderful word-pictures of this sunken land. Not a few old churches in this region were once built on islands, and approached by causeways. To this day, as one alights from Scrooby railway station, he notices, first of all, drains and culverts. As he walks to the village, past the old manor fields on the right, his pathway is upon timber raised above the oft-flooded road.

Since the great drainage operations in the form of canals, causeways, and dykes, made chiefly by the Dutch engineers in the seventeenth and eighteenth century, the whole face of the country has changed. The area of fertile soil having vastly increased, population has doubled, tripled, and quadrupled. Land once under water and given to breeding malarial diseases now smiles with grain and gardens, and is rich in cattle and men. Where two rabbits used to fight for one blade of grass, there are now a hundred stalks. John Wesley in 1703 opened his eyes on the island formed by three rivers, Trent, Idle, and Don, which in Pilgrim days was a pestilential marsh.

Vermuyden and his Dutchmen had drained it, making of it rich and dry soil. On Axelholme, once the swamp island, sprang up Epworth. To this day the Dutch accent and blood are noticeable in Lincolnshire. No region is more interesting to Americans than these eastern counties.

Study the names of places, and this part of England fronting Denmark and Friesland will tell stories as fascinating as fairy tales. Here has been the great battlefield of invading Briton, Roman, Anglo-Saxon, Frisian, and Dane. On every square mile they have fought, camped, or settled, made beacons on its hills, cut paths, and built roads. We recognize the names which each nation left behind it, and often as easily and as clearly as we tell the difference between the hoof-mark of a horse, the paw-print of a dog, and the track of a pigeon's pink toes. The Keltic "pen" and "combe" and "ock" appear and reappear. Count up the Roman's "castra" or camps, as in Doncaster, and note his "colonia," as in Lincoln. These and other Latin words have suffered a slight change of form. Of Anglo-Saxon names there is an abundance, as in "ham," which means home, such as Rotherham; in "field," such as Sheffield and Austerfield; and in "try," the name of a town, such as Coventry and Bawtry. After Frisians and Anglo-Saxons came the Danes, whose town names ended in "by" and "ing," as we see in Scrooby and Reading.

These Danes or Norsemen, our ancestors, were famous old pagans. Like the rest of their Scandinavian brethren, they remained "heathen" after the Frisians and Anglo-Saxons, both on the continent and in England, had become Christian. They worshiped Woden and Thor, whose names we preserve in Wednesday and Thursday. Woden was the god that knew everything, because two ravens, wisest of birds, flew out into all the world during the day, and came back at night to perch on his shoulder, and whisper in his ear, telling him everything. These ravens, Munin and Hugin, perception and reflection, helped to make Woden omniscient. When the Norsemen went out on the deep sea without chart or compass, they not only worshiped Woden, but honored the raven as his wise servant, using the bird at sea as a pilot, and on land as an indicator of the god's will. Very probably from this Norse mythology, Edgar A. Poe borrowed the idea of his talking bird, the raven of dark memory with its accusing "Nevermore."

The Danes were more than pirates. They were bold navigators, discoverers, and colonizers. Coming up the Humber and Trent rivers, they made this part of England especially theirs. They divided the country into "ridings," and enjoyed local government. Gainsborough is probably the place where Canute's followers wanted him to turn back the waters of the sea. Wherever the Danes got a foothold in England, there and only there do we find names of places ending in "by" and "ing," while other settlements of theirs have "raven" or "ran" in their names, such as Ranskill, the hamlet next to Scrooby; that is, the raven's knoll, or hill. It is not merely an accident that over the Austerfield church door are carved a dragon, the lightning zigzag of Thor, and the raven's beak of Woden's servants, conventional in form though they be.

These Norsemen, who were kinsmen of the later and more civilized Normans, not only robbed, burned, and killed, like our Saxon forefathers before them, but they loved to go into Christian churches to defile and burn them. But woe to them when they were caught! They were flayed alive, and their skins were fixed to the church doors. In more peaceful centuries bits of human skin found under the old nail-heads of oaken church doors have been deposited in the British Museum.

It is well to pay attention to these names, because like bones, nerves, and organs, whether of a man or a monkey, of a geological horse with toes or a modern horse with hoofs, as well as the features of plants and vegetables, they reveal early history, through heredity and evolution, far better than any later traditions or writings or orthodoxies possibly can do. They are original documents, which we can interpret without prejudice or heresy. To understand what kind of men and women lived in the Pilgrim district we must study their composite ancestry, the physiognomy of the country, and know the superstitions and beliefs of the people who lived on the soil. Neither Calvinism nor Puritanism nor Anglicanism can bleach out the stains of the primitive paganism of our Teutonic fathers. Just as the Spaniards chased the shadows of ancient myths in Florida and Mexico, so into North America Pilgrim and Puritan brought the legends and superstitions of northern Europe.

What we call the Pilgrim district is in the very heart of the Danish region. It lies chiefly along the steel tracks of the Great Northern Railway over which the lightning train called the "Flying Scotchman" whizzes on its way between London and Edinburgh. As on the silk threads of a double rosary, we can string most of the towns famous in Pilgrim story, either on this railway, or on the North Road, which, from Newark to Bawtry, at the end of Nottingham, is close to it. In Roman days the legions tramped towards the North Star, and the merchants transported their goods, over ground much the same, called the Fosse Way, or Ermine Street. In Elizabethan England, so soon as one got beyond the cities and towns, there were, roughly speaking, nothing better than unfenced paths. The highway to Scotland was little else than a horse track, though we shall find that it is the main geographical thread of our story. This horse track but a few feet wide, on which kings, nobles, and armies traveled, was called the Great Northern Road. It was the artery by which the people in this quiet agricultural region were connected with the mighty world beyond, through which they felt the throbs of England's life and the pulses of the continent.

The Pilgrim country is plain, and the scenery, though pretty, is not bold, striking, or romantic. It is mostly lowland, in the valleys formed by the Ryton and the Idle, — little rivers whose united flood helps to swell the Trent. Each of these three streams takes its source on the westward slopes of the famous Sherwood Forest. The Pilgrim district lies mostly in the valley of the southern Trent, which further north unites with the Ouse to form the river Humber. It was never very thickly populated, nor is it now, for its soil is not particularly fertile. Bawtry, the town lying between Austerfield and Scrooby, is one hundred and fifty-three miles north of London.

The Idle, which forms part of the boundary line between York and Notts, is usually a rushing stream and not at all lazy. Its name means "flowing through grain fields." The upper limit of the Pilgrim district is Austerfield. Take for its lower limit East Retford on the right, with Worksop (the home of the writer's ancestors) on the left, and we have a triangle, whose sides are, roughly, eleven, seven, and nine miles long. York, where the archbishop lived, was forty-six miles northward. Southward, Nottingham is thirty-five miles, and Newark upon Trent (where the writer's ancestor, Sir Gervaise Eyre, in command of the castle of King Charles I., was slain in the civil war), about twenty-five miles distant. Eastward, Gainsborough is twelve miles, Lincoln thirty-one miles, and Boston sixty-seven miles away.

The traveler must remember that the roads, as they now appear, are of modern construction. Such a thing as a wheeled wagon was quite uncommon in the early years of Henry VIII. Pleasure carriages were not seen until introduced from the continent. When the first one was driven abroad in London, people thought it was some Oriental shrine or curiosity. In all pictures and prints of the time, we see lords and ladies riding on horseback, but never in a carriage. "Palfrey," meaning an extra post-horse, was the common term for the animal carrying a lady. Fond of jewelry as they were in the age of Elizabeth, when the gold and spices and silks of the East and the wonderful things from America were getting to be well known in England, it was not uncommon to see "a lady on horseback" with peaked headdress, very long veil, skirts sweeping to the rear and upheld by pages, or even with "rings on her fingers and bells on her toes." Mother Goose's Melodies contain some very clear and very wonderful pictures of the England of long ago.

Scrooby and Austerfield, though small and mean places, were not the least among the northern villages. Near Austerfield is an old Roman earthwork linked with the name of the imperial general Ostorius, though the name (spelled Ousterfield in the Domesday book and Ansterfield in early Yankee printing) is most probably Teutonic for Easternfield.

Anglo-Saxon Austerfield had a little church in which a great question was settled for all Britain by a synod held in the year 702. A great controversy had arisen about the celebration of Easter. One party favored the British and the other the Roman date. Wilfrid, the handsome and eloquent Bishop of York, made a journey to Rome to find what the Pope thought. He was shipwrecked on the coast of Friesland, but the language on both sides of the North Sea being the same, he preached the gospel and introduced Christianity into the Netherlands. After seeing Rome, he returned to England and became a hot partisan of the southern style and time. He built many churches in England, but was always on the Roman side, taking his politics, as well as his dogmas, from the Tiber. He quarreled with

King Egfrid and his queen of Northumbria, who deposed him from the bishopric. He once more went to Rome and appealed to the Pope, who decided in his favor: but when he returned to England, the Saxon king snapped his fingers at the Italian bishop's decision, and imprisoned Wilfrid. He, however, escaped to Sussex, and there was successful as a missionary preacher. He still hoped to get back the bishopric of York, but even after Egfrid's death this king's father, Aldfrid, refused to reinstate the now aged prelate.

At the great synod which met at Austerfield in 702, King Aldfrid, the Archbishop Berthwald of Canterbury, and the bishops of almost all Briton assembled in this most central spot to hear the complaint of Wilfrid. Despite the pleadings of Wilfrid's brother, Archbishop of Canterbury, on his behalf, the king was sustained in his action. The synod of Austerfield excommunicated Wilfrid and his companions. So thoroughly was this work done that if any of the abbots or priests of Wilfrid's party said grace before meat in a man's house and signed the food with the sign of the cross, it was ordered to be cast forth as though offered to idols.

The pith and meaning of this ancient Austerfield matter is that in England the party backed by the Pope was beaten and the spirit of independence prevailed. The English won the day, preferring to regulate their religion in their own way. The twelve hundredth anniversary of this famous synod of Austerfield, which deposed Saint Wilfrid, will occur in 1902.

Nevertheless, Wilfrid got back his see before he died, and after his death this twice-deposed bishop and stanch upholder of Romish customs was canonized as a saint, while the church of Scrooby, built of stone, was named after him. It is Saint Wilfrid's church in which the Pilgrims first worshiped and which we see to-day.

In the Norman era, after the year 1088, Thomas of Bayeux became Archbishop of York. In crusading times, the lady Idorea de Vipont or her father, John de Busli, gave the whole village of Austerfield for the support of a chaplain to pray, and to celebrate, in the house at London, masses for the soul of Robert de Vipont. In the reign of Henry II. this John de Busli or Builli (1154–1189) built the new chapel at Austerfield, attaching it, as well as the chapel at Bawtry, to the convent at Blyth. The edifice was thus originally a "chantry," erected for the benefit of a "soul in purgatory." It is still standing and is called the Chapel of St. Helen. It was in this little house of worship, with its quaint port and double arched entrance carved with the Norsemen's symbols of the lightning's zigzag, raven's beak ornament, and a rude sort of dragon such as Saint George may have slain, that William Bradford was baptized March 19, 1590. Within the building some alterations, including new pews, have been made, but the outside of it was much the same as in Pilgrim days, until 1897, when a process of restoration began.

CHAPTER III

SCROOBY AND ITS HISTORY

SCROOBY was originally a Danish settlement, and had a close relationship with York, that wonderful place of Roman, Anglo-Saxon, Norman, and English fame. York is one of the most ancient of British cities, and was renowned for Jewish wealth as well as for clerical ambition. It had been the reputed birthplace of one Roman emperor, Constantine, the dwelling-place of another, Hadrian, and here Severus died. It was the seat of the first English parliament, and in this august body the abbot of the York monastery had a seat and wore a mitre. Though the archbishop dwelt in magnificence at York, he moved from place to place while attending to political and religious matters. At Scrooby was one of his summer palaces, hunting lodges, or places of abode, where he could also give lodging to his retainers.

In comparison with the cottages around it, the episcopal residence at Scrooby was a palace. Because it stood on a manor or estate owned by the prelate, it was also called a manor house, and in it on the 12th of January, 1535, there were thirty-nine chambers or apartments. According to an inventory there were in the great hall three screens, six tables, nine benches, and one cupboard. The furniture of the chapel consisted of a timber altar and two superaltars, or stone tops, to lay upon the wood, a reading-desk, a pair of organs, and a clock, possibly from Freiburg, but out of repair, lacking weights and cords. Shakespeare, in "Love's Labour 's Lost," makes Biron poke fun at the German clocks, "still a repairing; ever out of frame."

Probably the handsomest of all the apartments was the refectory, or dining-room, which was lined on ceiling and walls with carved oak panels and beams. The dining-chamber was "ceiled and dressed with 'wainscot,'" — which is an old Dutch word for the finest oak without knots or flaws. Many of these oaken beams are now to be found in the roof supports of the cow-houses and stables on the old site. As with most old castles and manors in those days, there was a moat or ditch around the four-sided inclosure, which was crossed by a drawbridge. The gate was on the east side. There were three fish-ponds, in which "Friday food" was kept swimming; for no meat was eaten on the day named after the old goddess Freyja, and on which Christ is believed to have been crucified.

Old John Leland, librarian and chaplain to Henry VIII., tells us about Scrooby of Tudor days. He received the king's commission to explore the cathedrals, colleges, abbeys and priories, and antiquities of his realm. He made a journey on horseback from Gainsborough westward over the Trent River into Nottinghamshire to the village of Mattersey. "Thence I rode a mile, in low wash and somewhat fenny ground; and a mile further or more by higher ground, to Scrooby." Besides the church, he "noted a great Manor Place . . . all builded of timber; saving the front of the hall, that is of brick, to which one ascends over cut-stone steps." After this, he forded the unbridged Ryton River, "and so betwixt the pales of two parks belonging to Scrooby," he came to Bawtry.

On this we may remark that probably the only bricks in the village were upon the Hall front. The rest of the edifice was of wood. The people's houses were of wattle, timber, and cement. Probably the only palings or fences were those of parks, belonging to rich landowners, who were at this time greedily encroaching upon the old common lands of the villages and taking away from the people what belonged to the public and not to the lords. In the latter part of the six teenth century things were going hard with the common people, especially with the agricultural workers. Phillip Stubbes, in 1583, complained bitterly of these landlords who were getting rich, not by stealing a goose from off the common, but by stealing the whole common from under the goose. In the six northern counties most of the land in the form of great estates was held by six families, and the farmers had an increasingly hard time, which made Pilgrim emigration more easy than it would have been if all had been well.

The church at Scrooby is named after the great Saint Wilfrid, so famous in England, Holland, and Rome, who was deposed, as we have seen, by the synod at Austerfield. It is built of cut square stones in what is called the early English and decorated style, with the crenelated walls rising above the edge of the roof. It has an eight-sided spire and four pinnacles, the five together representing the wounds of Christ. There are heads sculptured at the ends of the window mullions. On the east side of the church there seems to be what was once a leper window. Within, there is an aisle on the south side, but none to correspond with it on the north. Of the bells in the tower, one is of recent casting, and one was put there in 1647, but the other two bear the dates 1411 and 1511.

The tower, which has been twice struck by lightning during this century, is now equipped with a lightning rod such as Benjamin Franklin invented. The old oaken pews, which were carved in patterns representing vines, leaves, and grapes, lasted until about 1862. When the church was restored, and American lamps lighted with petroleum were put in, the old pews were sold for firewood, much to the grief of descendants of the Pilgrims who later tried to get the timber for souvenir material. Nevertheless, my friend Charles Carleton Coffin, of Boston, in 1890 secured from the parish clerk in the vicarage the old oaken box-desk, on which so long and so often lay the church register of baptism, marriage, and burial. It is carved in the same style of rude zigzag-and-beak carving, in Norman taste, which adorns the church porch at Austerfield. The desk is possibly as old as Saint Wilfrid's church itself.

In the churchyard there seems to be no tombstone older than 1620, and the parish registry does not go back even so far. Among the monuments in this God's acre is one to the memory of Archbishop Sandys' daughter. The arrangement of the tombs as we see them to-day has more respect to regularity of lines than to history or the bones beneath. To the northeast is the cottage known as the vicarage, where the parish clerk has for many generations lived. It is very plain, and inside there is a ladder by which one ascends to the upper floor.

Near by is the village pinfold, and within a few feet stood until lately the stocks, — one of the old-time institutions of every English village, the pound being intended for four-footed, and the stocks for two-footed transgressors of the law. Like the old font in which the young Pilgrims were baptized, the timber of the stocks was long since bought by Americans (for five pounds sterling). There is nothing now to be seen but the site whereon these stood.

I have visited Scrooby and the surrounding country four times, studying by day and night life in this little village, which has changed but slightly in three hundred years. There are two public houses, the "George and the Dragon," and "The Saracen's Head," where one can get refreshment for man and horse, but no lodging over night. On the morning of August 1, 1895, it was like seeing Gray's "Elegy" acted out before my eyes, as "the lowing herds wound slowly o'er the lea," after the "cock's shrill clarion" had been heard. In the fields the sheaves of cut grain were standing ready for the fork and wain, to be loaded and hauled into the barns. The birds were numerous and lively; so also were the August flies and the whirring beetles. In the grain fields I noticed that the plan was first to drive the mowing-machine along the outward edges, gradually approaching the centre. This, I found, was in order to force the rabbits into the last clump, where they could easily be killed and thus made ready for pie.

Where stood the old manor house is now a pasture, which by its lumpy and irregular surface shows to the eye skilled in studying old historic sites the lines of foundations long since hidden by overgrowing grass. Three circles, the sites of former fish-ponds, can be discerned. The moat has in some parts been entirely filled up and in others nearly so, while in no place is there more than a few feet of water. Horses and cows were grazing down in these ancient feudal boundaries and over the ridgy meadow.

All that is left of the ancient edifice is a portion of the modern house in which dwelt the postmaster of the village, Mr. David Shillito, who kept a record of American visitors and chatted freely of old times. He died at the age of seventy-six in 1896. The farm is held by a long lease from the Archbishop of York. This plain brick house, mostly of modern material and structure, has in one wall a lofty and round-headed arch, which is now filled in and may once have formed a coach-gate or carriage entrance to the manor house. On this house is now a bronze tablet affixed by grateful Americans. Going out into the stables and cow-houses, built of brick and holding up roofs of red tile, I saw many stout beams of carved oak. These, though dusty and cobwebbed, show that they were once used for a nobler purpose.

It is under a piece of one of these carved beams that I am writing this story of "The Pilgrims in their Three Homes." In the Massachusetts house at the World's Fair in Chicago, in 1893, this piece of English oak, cased in American glass and wood and duly inscribed, formed the starting-point for a tour of the various rooms which, in their furnishing and relics, showed the history of the old Bay State. Had it a tongue, it might be more definitely eloquent, and tell of many wonderful things which it had seen of Cardinal Wolsey and the archbishops. It might whisper how it had heard the prayers, the laughter, and the jests of gay lords and their retainers. It might also reëcho fervent petitions, heart-stirring sermons, and possibly the songs of the Pilgrim fathers, mothers, and children.

Scrooby, like an oft-touched bead slipped on the rosary of England's great northern high-road, has many precious associations.

It belonged to the Archbishops of York even when the Domesday book was written. Then "Scroobye" was only a "berrie" (bury), or hamlet, and William de Melton had "free warren" here. There must have been a lodge or building of some kind in the townlet in 1178, when John, the constable of Chester, granted to Roger, Archbishop of York, the town of Plumtree. Later on William Whorwood claimed twenty tofts, ten dovecotes, and twenty gardens here. In 1537 a successor in the line of York prelates demised to his brother, Geoffrey Lee, Plumtree Field, which was surrounded by palings, "besides

Scrooby Park, with the lodge upon the same, together with all his warren and game conies in the parishes of Scrooby and Haworth for forty-one years."

A word about warrens. From the most ancient times down to these years of grace, the English folk have always enjoyed hunting and eating the conies or rabbits as mentioned in the bequest. By the law of 1539 it was felony "to take in the king's ground any egg or bird . . . or to kill any conies or rabbits . . . or to enter . . . to kill and steal any conies."

It was at Scrooby that Archbishop Gray, in 1232, wrote to the brethren of the Hospital of St. John, Nottingham, a letter which is still extant. Here also, in 1530, came Cardinal Wolsey, whom some call "the greatest political genius England ever produced." After having studied the hearts of men, he was glad to commune with nature, and to muse over the fickleness of princes' favors. He had been Archbishop of York by title sixteen years before visiting the province over which he was placed. He spent three months at Scrooby before going to the chief city of his see. He died at Leicester, November 29, 1530. Among his last written words was a request to the king "to depress this new pernicious sect of the Lutherans."

CHAPTER IV

NOTTINGHAM AND THE ROBIN HOOD COUNTRY

THE county or shire of Nottingham is not varied and hilly like Derby, its famous neighbor on the west. Its climate is much dryer, for it lies just out of the influence of those great hill-ranges which form the backbone of England and attract the rain clouds. The name "Nottingham" means the home of dens or caves. These, excavated out of the New Red Sandstone series of rocks, are very numerous in its southern portion.

Dull as it looks to the traveler seeking bold scenery, this is the county of Maid Marian, and of Robin Hood, Friar Tuck, Little John, and the other gay fellows who lived in Sherwood Forest. It is the scene of Sir Walter Scott's "Ivanhoe," and of Arthur Sullivan's opera of the same name. To be sure, nobody knows whether such persons having those particular names ever lived, though something like documentary proof of the existence of Robin Hood is not wholly lacking. To have been in English prose and poetry for over six hundred years, and to be read about in one of the first books printed in England, makes rather respectable antiquity. It was

"The Little Jest of Robin Hood" in which the English people at large first saw their native language put in type, by the Dutch printer Wynken de Worde and his compositors and pressmen. This booklet contained a string of popular ballads. It was the "libretto" of a sort of rustic opera, a widespread annual celebration of country sports and masquerading, in which the fat friar, the expert archer, the tall John, and the pretty maid were gayly represented. With this came to be associated all sorts of merry games, athletics, dances, and masquerades, often coarse and even lewd. The fun, the songs, and the dances extended through Nottingham into other counties. This annual "epidemic of rapture" gave the reformers much trouble to put down. No doubt the young folk of Scrooby enjoyed the lively revels, and the Puritan leaders had hard work to stop the excesses. On the other hand, King James, who hated "Papists, Puritans, and Precisians," in the "Dance Book" of 1618 allowed May-games, Whitsun ales, Morris dances, leaping, vaulting, and acrobatic shows on Sunday afternoons to all those who would attend the state church. It is right here in this county of Notts that we find more about Robin Hood and the places made famous by him, or the legends about him, than in any other shire of England.

Scrooby is in the district of "Basset Law." The old Danish term "law" means something fixed or set, whether a custom, a writing, or a hill. It is often applied to rising or strikingly visible ground, hard and immovable. All through North England and Scotland this word "law" refers to a hill, especially one standing alone and not in ranges. Probably the most remarkable natural feature in the "flat and featureless" north half of Notts is this Berset or Basset Hill. Long ago it was called the Basset Law or "lawe," which has given its name to the "hundred."

This division of the land was made by the Germanic tribes which settled England. As a unit of arrangement it was originally based on the number of fighting men furnished. Ten tithings of freeholders made a "hundred," and ten families a "ton," or town. The "hundred" afterwards became the basis of taxes and other financial and political matters. In the divisions of land in America, the systems varied, but there were the "hundreds" in Pennsylvania, Virginia, Maryland, and Delaware. In the Chesapeake Bay State they served as election districts. In the State of Delaware they were retained longest.

Nottingham produces coal, but it is far down below the surface. It was long after the Pilgrims went away that the coal measures were reached by drilling under the overlying strata of clay. By this application of science coal mines were opened and developed and new industries were established; and now Nottingham laces, curtains, and stockings have become as household words in every land where English is spoken.

The sixteenth century seemed a very wonderful one to our fathers. Great changes took place within the four countries in the British Isles, both in politics, religion, and commerce. Drake ploughed "the first English furrow round the world." England began to influence more and more potently other nations, and to be more and more influenced by them. Henry VIII. broke with the Pope of Rome, and Italian power in England largely ceased. The old monasteries, of which there were a great many in Northern England, — Scrooby being in the midst of a large circle of them, — were suppressed. A few schools were founded in their place, but most of the lands, revenues, and buildings having been made by act of Parliament the property of the king, were made over by him to his favorite nobles. This high-handed act of the king was not a movement in favor of the people. The people, not having been educated in the Reformed faith, did not take kindly to the change from Romanism to that semi-reformation which afterwards became Anglicanism. Many famous families and men, like Miles Standish's kin at Duxbury Hall, in Lancashire, and Milton's grandfather and brother, remained Roman Catholics.

There was more than one great uprising in Lincolnshire against Earl Cromwell and the king's authority. "The Pilgrimage of Grace" in 1536 was attended with riot and bloodshed, and so was "The Rising of the North" in 1569. The people had liked the old customs and privileges, doles and charities, to which they had become used under the monastic system, and they wanted them again. They clamored for the "Sunday of joy," the hot cross buns, the dances and sports, the stories and jokes from the pulpit at Easter, the shining cross set up in the rood loft between the nave and the chancel, the church ales and glutton masses, the colors and varied dresses of the priests and monks, and the enjoyable good things which had been swept away along with some which they were not sorry to see go. The first insurrection was put down by King Henry VIII. with an iron hand. "The whole country was covered with gibbets."

The second insurrection, which gathered an army at Doncaster, expected aid from Spain, but did not get it. Elizabeth in her severe punishments showed herself the daughter of Henry VIII., the memorials whereof still lie on the landscape. "Gibbet Hill" and "Hangman's Lane," not far from Scrooby, tell their own story. The ancient Greeks erased every sign of ill-omen and memorial of disaster from the landscape, but the "Anglo-Saxon" people in both England and America seem to delight in things ugly and gloomy, and befoul much lovely scenery with hideous names. The English people had to become accustomed to the new order of things, which in the end was for their benefit, but the change from the Roman to the Reformed religion went on slowly.

In those times it was customary for the sheriff of Yorkshire to come to Bawtry, the county boundary-line, for "Scrooby water divideth the shires," there meet the king when he was traveling north, and escort him over the border. So when Bluff King Hal came to Bawtry in 1541, it was necessary for the noblemen and the yeomen of all that region to show that they were loyal to him and were sorry for the late rebellion called "The Pilgrimage of Grace." It was a grand sight when "two hundred gentlemen of the country in velvet, and four thousand tall yeomen and serving men well horsed . . . on their knees made a submission by the mouth of Sir Robert Bowes and presented the King with £900." A similar scene I have witnessed, when two thousand feudal retainers of the Prince of Echizen, all robed in silk, fell on their knees before their lord, in the great castle halls at Fukui, Japan, presenting their gifts and assurances of fealty.

King Henry's wastefulness entailed great poverty and distress upon the people. A large demand for wool and sheep led to the inclosing of the pastures on common land which had always been practically the property of the people. Under Elizabeth things were improved in every way, but more particularly for the benefit of the people living in towns and cities than for the farming communities. Her ambition was to unite the throne and the people, to weaken the power of the nobles, to introduce arts and manufactures, to improve the currency, to welcome foreigners who were skilled mechanics or persons of craft and talent. She compelled each family of the tens of thousands from the Netherlands who had come into her realm to take an English apprentice, so that the country might immediately get the benefit of continental superiority in science, art and handicraft. In this way England was quickly changed from a purely agricultural to a manufacturing country, though the weaving, dyeing, fulling of cloth, and the various processes made use of in working glass, iron, pottery, metals, and wood were carried on, not in large factories, but in private houses, exactly as I saw was the case in the Japan of 1870. Elizabeth personally encouraged these industries. Her visits to manufacturing towns, notably one to Norwich, were long famous for artificers' pageants and industrial tableaux.

The Virgin Queen was strenuous in making everything uniform in church and state. Her one idea was to make England great. In her eyes religion was a method in politics. Whether at heart Elizabeth was a Protestant or a Papist, Romish or Reformed, no man knoweth unto this day. This queen, called " that bright Occidental Star " by those who saluted King James as " the Sun," certainly treated the Puritans even more roughly than she treated the Catholics. Her economic methods were of benefit to manufacturers, but did not improve the condition of the farm laborers. After keeping off war with Spain by means of her diplomacy for thirty years, she agreed to help the Dutch republic and thus to have the actual fighting done on the continent. Brave little Holland was England's outer dike of defense.

With ten thousand English, Welsh, Irish, and Scottish soldiers, fighting under the red, white, and blue flag of the republic, thousands of British contractors, merchants, traders, and agents in the Low Countries, and a hundred thousand Netherlanders, mostly educated people and skilled workmen, in the British Isles, relations between England and Holland were close and varied. Through enlarged commerce, the English people began to enjoy abundantly what had been curiosities for the rich. These were new vegetables and other articles of food, gay and substantial clothing, starch and white linen goods, bricks and brick houses, improved ploughs, pleasure carriages, well-made wagons, carpets, looking-glasses, and ten thousand new and wonderful comforts and novelties which made life, not only in English towns and cities, but also in the rural districts, very different from what it had been in the days of Robin Hood, or in the fifteenth century.

Southern and especially eastern England was most rapidly and thoroughly affected by these changes for the better. It is out of the eastern counties, until quite modern times, that most of England's men of civil abilities and military power, and her chief wealth, have come. The western counties were more famous for their ships and sailors. In northern England the population was sparse, and the people more rude and ignorant. There were few schools. Education was very backward. The Roman Catholic spirit was much stronger than in the freer south. The people were more attached to the monks and lords, the castles and monasteries. The great mass of population, as well as of wealth, was in the southern shires, where the people were peaceful, progressive, and up to the times. There was a bitter sectional feeling between the north and the south, the poorer and more priest-ridden northerners envying the wealth and comfort of the more commercial southerners. So far back as 1361 we find Queen Margaret moving with an army on London, only to be beaten by Edward IV. at the battle of Towton. "The Pilgrimage of Grace" in 1537 and "the Uprising of the North" in 1569, which were animated with the same envy, were the last attempts of the north forcibly to express opposition to the south.

Until about 1590, then, the people of northern Nottingham, and of the little hook of Yorkshire which comes into Notts, lived their quiet lives, unvexed by the great world without, though they had excitement enough at home with the "bruits," and the uprisings, and the royal armies sent to suppress these, whenever words of complaint turned to acts of violence. America had been discovered by the Venetian Cabot sailing from Bristol in 1497, nearly a century before, but fifty years went by before the fact was popularly known, or any allusion had been made to it in an English book. What we Americans know so well about Sir Walter Raleigh's attempts to colonize the Carolinas was almost unheard of in northern England, for most of Raleigh's colonists were Irishmen and southerners.

Of many of the counties in England we may say that they were, from the point of view of farm laborers, almost like foreign countries, having different dialects, manners, customs, ideas, and superstitions. The general condition of the people in the northern counties was much like that of the mountain whites of "Appalachian America" fifty years ago. In these people of the plateau formed by western North Carolina and eastern Kentucky and Tennnesee, we see our "contemporary ancestors," who still use about two hundred old English expressions which are obsolete elsewhere, and which uneducated Britons think are "Americanisms."

CHAPTER V

WILLIAM BREWSTER

MEN believe that they are hearing the Divine Voice when they are called to reform manifest abuses. So felt the English Puritans of the sixteenth century, among whom were those who later became Separatists. In the development in northern England of the Pilgrims, we may discern five notable factors. These were the Bible in English, the presence of the Anabaptists in England, the visit of William Brewster to the Netherlands, the coming at Brewster's invitation of three other Cambridge men into the Pilgrim district, and the system of inclosures for sheep pastures, which made farming a losing occupation, and so inclined many plain people to emigrate. The leaders of the movement in Gainsborough and Scrooby were four men, Brewster, Robinson, Clifton, and Smyth, each of whom had been trained in Cambridge University. The first and greatest of them was Brewster, and the next was Robinson.

In English intellectual history Oxford has stood for privilege, royalty, high churchism, things conservative, and faith in things as they are and have been, — the safe side. This was the prevailing sentiment and feeling in the middle counties of England, which were not so easily influenced by the continent or the ocean and foreign commerce. On the other hand, Cambridge has stood for the people, for freedom and progress, and for the truth, not only that has been, but which is and is to be. Cambridge is the product of, and has profoundly influenced, eastern England. It is in close and living touch with that great region from Lincolnshire to Kent, between the backbone of England's central hills and the German Ocean. Cambridgeshire borders those counties of Essex, Suffolk, and Norfolk, which have ever been quick to respond to the fertilizing ideas, commerce, and intellectual movements of continental Europe. It is closest to Holland, from which it has borrowed most of her republican ideas. This region of country is very homelike to Americans, because of familiar names and idioms, and as the birthplace of so many of their ancestors. We could not imagine a Pilgrim movement starting from Oxford, especially from sixteenth-century Oxford, where during one of its many reactions Cranmer, Latimer, and Ridley were burned. It is easier to think that to Cambridge, far more than to Oxford, the United States and the world owe immeasurable debts of gratitude.

The man who emerges as the beginner of the Pilgrim movement was William Brewster, whose father had charge of the relay station or post at

Scrooby, and who was born before 1567. He grew up in the village, seeing whatever came into the place from the great world outside. When the king's messengers changed horses, drank their ale, or took their supper and breakfast at his father's inn, he was apt to hear news. Occasionally some gay or even royal lady would pass that way. Margaret, Queen of Scotland, daughter of King Henry VII., slept at Scrooby on the 12th of June, 1503, on her way northward. Perhaps as a great curiosity, new and strange, the young Brewster would see a man burning tobacco in a bowl, and "drinking the smoke," as people used to say in those days. He little realized then that he would one day be a cultivator of the weed in its home-land beyond the Atlantic. After he had been to school somewhere in the neighborhood, probably at Bawtry, he went to Cambridge. It is not at all improbable that he walked the whole way thither. Thirteen of the seventeen colleges now forming the university were then in existence. Brewster entered Peterhouse, the oldest college of all, founded in 1284, and made his first record, December 3, 1580. An English college in those days was much like some of our smaller "universities,"—little more than a grammar school. Though it is quite probable that Brewster did not graduate or take a degree, yet he was long enough at Cambridge to come under the influences of the Puritan preachers, and to become most decidedly earnest in his Christian character.

Brewster was called away from his studies to help William Davison, who had long been Elizabeth's envoy at Antwerp. Davison had in 1583 traveled from London to Scotland, which was then to an Englishman like a foreign country, and so continued to be until after Cromwell's time. It is almost a certainty that Davison stopped at Scrooby inn, where he may have met young Brewster, then about sixteen or seventeen. Davison was on royal business, to head off an alliance which the French wanted to make with the Scottish King James VI. When in 1585 Elizabeth finally concluded to join forces with the Dutch United States in order to help the cause of freedom, and keep the Spaniards occupied and away from England, Davison was dispatched as her envoy to negotiate terms, for the thrifty queen wanted to be sure of getting back the money loaned. Holland and Zealand were in reality fighting England's battle, and the States were paying her troops, yet she acted more like a usurer than a friend, requiring them to deliver up two towns and a fort as security. These were to be garrisoned by English governors, and to be put under martial law. Under Providence it was this arrangement that gave not only Sir Philip Sidney to Holland, but Miles Standish to America. The English garrisons were maintained even during seven years of the Twelve Years' Truce, 1609–1621.

Just as the Japanese submitted to the humiliation of "extraterritoriality" for over forty years, so did the Dutch Republicans for thirty-one years (until Barneveldt's masterly statesmanship relieved them), since it was a matter of life and death with them to get English aid. So they handed over at once, in token of their good faith, the great iron keys of the city gates of Flushing on the Scheldt, Brill on the Maas, and the fort of Rammekens on Walcheren. This island, owing to the fact that so many fine vegetables and table delicacies, then practically unknown in England, were imported thence, came to be called "Queen Elizabeth's kitchen garden." These keys of the "cautionary towns" were ponderous affairs, and were held on a great iron ring. They were so heavy that Davison could not well carry them around with him. So he gave them in charge of the young college boy, Brewster, who proudly slept with them at night under his pillow. Probably the young Puritan was familiar with the text in Isaiah xxii. 22.

Davison had long lived in Antwerp, where his children were born, and where he was an elder in an English Puritan church. The Pilgrims were not the first Englishmen who fled to the Low Countries for freedom's sake, for there were English churches at Antwerp, Middelburg, and Embden, as well as in other places on the continent, such as Frankfort and Geneva, where the Puritan parties formed their opinions and polity, and made the popular English Bible. Davison knew the freedom of thought, religion, and publishing in the democratic Netherlands, and his influence in training Brewster was excellent. The female ruler of England generally followed very good advice when she listened to Davison, who told her truly what kind of people the Dutch were, though he thereby shocked those insular prejudices, so many of which Americans have foolishly inherited.

The relations between Davison and Brewster must have been very close and even affectionate. Bradford declares that Davison trusted Brewster above all that were about him, and employed him in all matters of greatest trust and secrecy, esteeming him rather as a son than a servant. In private he talked with him more like a friend than a master, and thought much of the lad because of his wisdom and godliness.

Landing at Vlissingen, or "Flushing," as English people call the port city of Zealand, the Puritan master, Davison, and his young servant, Brewster, rode to Middelburg, at which city the Pilgrim story may, in a very important sense, be said to have begun. Here the Anabaptists were first in Europe given liberty of conscience, and here Robert Browne, besides finding asylum and toleration, printed and issued his books which first taught in English the Congregational idea of church government. Within the period of six score years, between stadholder and great-grandson, the toleration secured in the Netherlands by William the Silent, in 1577, and in England under William III. of "ever blessed memory," in 1688, lies the story of the beginning and maturing of the Pilgrim enterprise. In short, the definite epoch of the Pilgrims in their three homes fills a little more than a century. Brewster entered Holland just after the death of the man whom the Dutch called Father of his Country, and Plymouth Colony ceased when William III. became King of England.

It must have been a wonderful experience for this bright young Englishman to travel in a state so highly civilized as Holland, which then was in many respects, especially in social refinement and the comforts of life, far superior to Brewster's native country. He saw gayly dressed and well-fed people in many walled cities, excellent farms, well-made and well-kept roads, noble church edifices, superb city halls, dwellings built of brick, and striking cleanliness everywhere, while the carillons of bells in the spires doubtless pleased his ear.

We may be sure that so observing and keen-minded a man as Brewster afterwards showed himself to be could not fail to notice especially those things which were very different from what one could find in the England of his time, such as the federal union of seven states, self-government of cities, judges independent of the executive, the democratic spirit of the churches, public schools for the youth and free instruction to poor children, the freedom of the press, and the liberty of printing and publishing. He could not but note the toleration granted to Roman Catholics, Jews, Anabaptists, and other people without the state church. These "dissenters," though not allowed public processions or parades, or crosses or symbols on the outside of their places of worship, were perfectly free indoors and suffered no molestation. The great number of people able to read and write, of cheap books and pictures, of schools, hospitals, orphan asylums, and benevolent institutions, must have impressed Brewster; while the number and variety of manufactures, the gayety of the markets, the vast fisheries and tremendous commerce, — proportionally so much greater than anything then known in his own country, — opened his eyes to the wonderful world beyond his native island. Above all, this idea of liberty of conscience, the devoutness and earnestness of the Dutch Puritans, and the determination of all, Protestants and Catholics alike, to fight Spain until their freedom was acknowledged, must have kindled new thoughts in the mind of William Brewster.

How the English and Irish troops, led by Robert Dudley, Earl of Leicester, landed at Flushing and marched to the Hague, amid bonfires, pageants, fireworks, and every sort of civic rejoiing, can be seen in the Dutch picture galleries, and read in Leicester's correspondence and the state papers of both countries. The Netherlanders are famous for making calls on New Year's Day, a custom which Dutchmen introduced into the American United States. Davison, and possibly young Brewster, was present during that memorable call on New Year's morning of January 14, 1586, when the deputies of the States-General offered the earl the absolute government of the Low Countries. Strange as it may seem, the democratic and Calvinistic forces rallied around Leicester, while the aristocratic and state-rights elements gathered about Barneveldt.

Leicester's head was turned by such an honor and he accepted. Sidney and Davison did not dissuade him from doing this, though it was in direct violation of Elizabeth's command, and woefully did the queen make her servant rue his presumptuous act. With vast pomp Leicester was installed governor and captain-general of the Union of states on February 6. Instead of his dispatching explanations to the queen much sooner, especially as a fair wind was blowing, Davison was not sent from the Hague until February 5. He was to sail at once from Brill, but he and Brewster were detained by stormy weather five or six days, so that they did not arrive in London until February 13.

Long before this, Elizabeth had heard that the Countess of Leicester was about to join the earl in Holland, with a train of ladies, and such rich "coaches, litters, and side-saddles" as should make a court which would surpass her own. This made the jealous queen furious and stirred her to "extreme choler and dislike of all the earl's proceedings." With strong language she declared she would have "no more courts under her obeisance than her own." Davison on his arrival had to hear the queen's wrath against both himself and Leicester, and later the ungrateful earl managed to throw most of the blame, which his own folly deserved, upon Davison. But the latter defended himself with spirit; and the treaty with Scotland having been concluded successfully on the 17th of July, and the Scottish commissioners dismissed in good humor, Walsingham wrote to Leicester on July 22 that Elizabeth "seemeth to be disposed to make Mr. Davison my assistant in the place I serve." This she did, though the warrant was not issued until the 12th of December, 1586. Part of Davison's business while in office was to effect the transportation from Ireland to the Netherlands of a further contingent of one thousand Irishmen, as part of the British forces fighting for freedom.

When he came back after a year's absence,

Brewster was no longer merely a country lad or college student.

The Dutch United States had honored Davison, as they usually did the foreign envoys that pleased them, with a gold chain. Arriving in England, Davison put this gold chain on young Brewster as his own charge, and commanded him to wear it as they rode through the country till they came into the queen's presence.

The episode of William Brewster's presence in Holland at a critical period in Dutch history, and during the movement of the Calvinistic democratic and unionist elements in the federal republic, which Davison could not but favor, is of great significance to the philosophic student of Pilgrim history. Brewster must then and there have seen clearly the difference between the forces making for the uplifting of the common people and the consolidation of a strong and united nation, and those which nourished aristocracy, privilege, and wealth, and even secession. Evidently he went back to his old home mightily reinforced in heart and intellect. His whole after life shows what principles he followed — even those which have made the better life of England, Holland, and the United States of America.

As early as November 15, Davison, as the queen's secretary, wrote to Earl Leicester, expressing Her Majesty's great grief for the loss at Zutphen of Sir Philip Sidney, whose elegant

Latin has supplied the motto of that great State of Massachusetts, of which Brewster was to lay the foundation-stone.

Remaining from the autumn of 1586 until February, 1587, with Davison, who was during this time in daily attendance upon the queen, the young man Brewster must have seen a good deal of English court life. All seemed to be going well with him, and he was apparently destined to become a shining figure in political life, either at court, in parliament, or on some foreign embassage.

But a woman was destined to change the current of the Scrooby lad's career, to be the innocent cause of Davison's disgrace, to cause a controversy which has not yet been settled, and indirectly to be one of the makers of the Pilgrim community and of New England. This was none other than the beautiful Mary Stuart, Queen of Scots. Elizabeth Tudor believed that she must put Mary to death, thinking her own throne and her country were not safe while the adherents of Rome had hopes of a living leader. Elizabeth, however, who was as unscrupulous as she was brave, and who always sought to have a scape-goat on whom she could throw any odium which might come from her own acts, selected Davison as her beast of evil burden. She first allowed her wrath to explode upon him, and then drove him into the Tower solitudes.

In February, 1587, it was published abroad that the Scottish queen had been beheaded. Davison was then imprisoned, and Brewster returned to live with his father at Scrooby. As a popular and beloved friend and gentleman, his true character shone as brightly in the country village as at court or in foreign lands. His father's health was failing, and young Brewster did the real work at the relay station, as his father and grandfather had done before him. Although the royal postmaster-general in London wanted to appoint one of his own relatives, a lawyer of Gray's Inn, to the vacant position, and all the more because young Brewster was not that kind of an office-seeker that flatters men who have patronage to dispense, yet though largely through Davison's earnest exertions, William Brewster was appointed as post at Scrooby on the great North Road to Scotland. It was most probably about this time that he married.

There were four of these posts, or royal routes from London, three of which went towards foreign countries, and one to the place whence distant voyages were most frequent. The first led to the north into the foreign country of Scotland; the second westward to Anglesea and across the Irish Sea to Ireland; the third southward to Dover and the continent; and the fourth to Plymouth, where was the chief naval station. The method of the posts was much like that which

I saw and used in 1871 in Japan. It was not like our "pony express" over the Western plains, before the days of railways, in that it was very much slower. It was for travel and the exchange of horses rather than for the carrying of letters.

With other perquisites, Brewster's salary amounted to about fifteen hundred dollars a year, at a time when money was worth four times what it is now, thus making fine pay. This enabled him to entertain, often at his own charges, as Bradford tells us, the whole Pilgrim company to dinner, when they would come to the manor house for worship. Some of these earnest people walked from two to twenty miles for this purpose. Among them was one, Gervaise Nevell, who, as I have good reason for believing, was a kinsman to my own ancestors. He was destined to be the first Pilgrim caught, imprisoned, and summoned before the court at York for "Brownism." He afterwards fled to Amsterdam.

From the first, Brewster was the soul of the Pilgrim company, and this was before any Puritan minister who was also a Separatist had come into the region. Throughout his adult life he was the generous provider, the nursing father of the Pilgrim church. Yet one would not appreciate him rightly who did not pay proper tribute also to his intellectual abilities and personal influence. From first to last, as must not be forgotten, the Pilgrim church, like the very first Christian churches, was not only composed of, but was served and managed by laymen, — a majority of the congregation of believers forming the simple and sufficient government, under Christ their only over-lord and master. As the Pilgrims read the New Testament, they found in it no trace of a clerical caste. Neither did they discover power in any corporation, ecclesiastical or political, outside of the congregation, that insures validity of ordination. Brewster not only found freedom of conscience in the Bible, but at Scrooby he published the news of a country which practiced and guaranteed it.

CHAPTER VI

WILLIAM BRADFORD

NEXT to Brewster the chief man of the Pilgrim company, taking all things into consideration, was William Bradford, who was baptized March 19, 1590, and was brought to baptism by Henry Fletcher, who made the record in the register. Bradford's father was a yeoman, and died when the boy was about a year old.

After his father's death young Bradford was put under the care of his grandfather, who died when he was about six years old. He was then brought up by his three uncles, William, Thomas, and Robert Bradford. William's grandfather and old William Bradford were the two subsidy-men, or tax collectors, at Austerfield, and when young Bradford's uncle Robert died, his will showed that he owned an iron-bound wagon, while in his "house," which in old country English means the sitting, or "living" room, were a cupboard and a long settee, or bench. He had also armor and leases of land. His acquaintances and connections show that he was one of the most important persons in the village. If the tradition that the dwelling pointed out in Austerfield to-day as the home of Bradford be correct, then in the fact that they lived in a brick house — poor and small though it seem to us — we have a further argument to show that the Bradfords were of importance and of high character. Brewster was twenty-three years old when Bradford was born, which was on the day that the former was appointed post of Scrooby.

Bradford grew up in the village, the centre of which was the little chapel. He had a long sickness, which left him a delicate boy, and helped to fit him to become the serious man that he afterwards was. Even when about a dozen years old, the reading of the Scriptures fed his imagination and made a profound impression upon his mind. Very probably, after learning to read, he gained what knowledge he could from the books of the Rev. Mr. Silvester, of Alkly, the guardian of his cousins, who had not only some land, but also an English and Latin library.

Bradford's impressions were much assisted and improved when he heard the preaching of the Rev. Richard Clifton at Babworth, about ten miles away, to whose church and rectory Bradford no doubt often walked.

Dr. Cotton Mather, who tells us these things, says that Bradford was further befriended by being brought into the company and fellowship of earnest Christian young men, though one of those who at first most influenced him afterwards became profane and wicked. He adds: "Nor could the wrath of his uncles, nor the scoff of his neighbors, now turned upon him as one of the Puritans, divert him from his pious inclination. . . . He set himself by reading, by discourse, by prayer, to learn whether it was not his duty to withdraw from the communion of the parish assemblies, and to engage with some society of the faithful that should keep close unto the written Word of God, as the rule of their worship."

As a true Christian soldier Bradford learned early to stand fire. After much mental distress he resolved to give up going to the state church, and began to attend as regularly as possible the meetings of those Christians who took only the written Word for their rule of life, without regard to politicians, whether lay or clerical. At Gainsborough and Scrooby he found the food which his spirit craved. "And the sudden deaths of the chief relations which thus lay at him quickly after convinced him . . . and so to Holland he attempted a removal." As surely as Abraham listened to the Divine voice, so Bradford and his yoke-fellows heard this call, "Wherefore come out from among them, and be ye separate, said the Lord, and touch not the unclean thing; and I will receive you, and will be a Father unto you, and ye shall be my sons and daughters, saith the Lord Almighty."

We do not know, and can but guess that tradition is possibly correct in hinting that for Bradford, at least, one of the attractions at church was the pretty face of the girl whom years afterwards he married in America. What English maids in their beauty are, we know well by sight and not merely by faith. What they were in Bradford's day we learn from Erasmus. Does he not tell us that they were "divinely fair"? and well did this Rotterdammer know. No need for them to paint their cheeks of damask and rose; for as a German traveler once said of English ladies, "They do not heretic their faces."

Let us now look at those Puritan ministers who gave up their livings under the political establishment in order to serve a church founded on the primitive New Testament model. The first was Richard Clifton, originally from Derby, the next county to Notts. He was thirty-three years old when he came, probably at Brewster's invitation or through his influence, to Babworth, July 12, 1586. He showed himself to be an advanced preacher who believed thoroughly in the necessity of reforming the church. His field of labor was among the farmers and farm laborers, for his church was in the country where there was not even a village. Bradford speaks of him in the highest terms. Another Nottinghamshire man and Cambridge graduate, the Rev. Richard Bernard, was made vicar of Worksop June 19, 1601. Before this, in 1598, Bernard had been in charge of the rectory at Epworth, on the river island of Axelholme, in Lincolnshire, where John Wesley was born and which is now the Mecca of the Methodists, American and British. Thus in one small district of northern England, wherein, one generation before the Pilgrim movement, the people had risen in rebellion to preserve the corrupt church and the monasteries, we find the beginnings of three great bodies of Christians, — three folds of the "one flock, one Shepherd."

Besides being a Puritan, Bernard was ready to be a Separatist. He worked with Clifton and Brewster, his neighbors, and went so far as to set up a Congregational church within his parish and edifice.

The Scrooby brethren fully expected him to be one who through good and evil report would follow them to the goal of scriptural freedom. It turned out differently. When persecution, imprisonment, and death showed beyond a doubt that episcopacy was to be established by military force, and when Bernard was silenced by the Archbishop of York, then he drew back, and, conforming to the state church, wrote books against his former fellow workers. Whether he did this from lack of moral stamina, or from fondness for literary dalliance, or whether he was actuated by a sincere conviction of duty, God knows. *Deo Vindice!* It was in answer to the charges of the vicar at Worksop that John Robinson wrote his most famous book, "A Justification of Separation from the Church of England."

On the other side of the Trent, in Lincolnshire, Puritan sentiments among ministers who did not approve of the Romish ceremonies retained in the church were in some respects even more forward than in Nottingham. A Congregational church was formed at Gainsborough in 1602, probably meeting in the old Guild Hall, which is still standing. Brewster, Bradford, and those who with them had walked over from Scrooby met often with the people of this church. Their bishop, or pastor, was John Smyth, who had taken his degree at Christ's College, Cambridge, having for one of his tutors Francis Johnson, afterwards pastor of the Separatist church in London and Amsterdam. Johnson suffered for his faith at the hands of the rulers of England in this time of spiritual twilight. He fled to Amsterdam in 1606.

About 1606 the brethren at Scrooby and on the western side of the Trent formed a church, of which the Rev. Richard Clifton, late rector at Babworth, became pastor. This church was organized like those of the early Christians, by the free choice of the people, who elected their own officers, voting not by written ballot, as in Friesland, but by the holding up of hands. Beside the teaching members of the congregation, usually called clergymen, and in some branches of the

Christian church made into a separate caste, there were the serving members or deacons. Clifton continued to be the chief bishop, or pastor, and John Robinson the assistant bishop, or pastor.

This John Robinson, one of the makers of distinctive America, was born, probably in Gainsborough, certainly in Lincolnshire, and went to Corpus Christi College in Cambridge, in 1592, entering as a freshman when but seventeen years old. He took his degree and was made fellow in 1598. He settled at Norwich, but he preached in a way that led to his suspension. Then separating from the Establishment ruled by the queen, he became pastor of a Congregational church in Norwich about 1601 or 1602. So many Dutch Anabaptists and martyrs under "Bloody Mary" had been burned here, in the dry moats at the foot of the old Norman castle, that firewood became dear and the poor suffered from the cold.

In this city, as is very probable, Robert Browne, also educated at Corpus Christi College in Cambridge, usually reputed to be "the founder of modern Congregationalism," probably got his first ideas of primitive Christianity from the Dutch Anabaptists, and his followers were called "Brownists." This word was for over a century a common term in English speech. Shakespeare makes one of his characters say, "I had as lief be a Brownist as a politician." Browne, in 1580 or

1581, organized a church in Norwich; but finding his limbs and life in danger, he fled to Zealand, then the most intensely Protestant state in all Europe. In Middelburg, he printed tracts and books which were smuggled into England and circulated by two of his fellow believers, Coppin and Thacker. These, when caught by the authorities, in 1583, were hanged.

It was surely not an accident that both Robert Browne and John Robinson, while settled in Norwich among the Dutch Anabaptists, who held to the congregational principles of church polity, should learn from them and become like them. Robinson neither liked nor took the name of "Brownist" any more than that of "Anabaptist," both being terms of reproach. Like the Brethren themselves, both Browne and Robinson contended that in the Scriptures alone were found the source of their light and the basis of their church polity.

An argument against the idea that Browne learned the way from the "Anabaptists" has been attempted to be based on the fact that the names of Browne's co-workers are not distinctively Dutch; but from this nothing can be argued, because most of the Dutch, like the Walloons and the Huguenot emigrants to England, quickly translated, shortened, assimilated to English sound, or otherwise anglicized their names. De Wilde became Savage; van de Velde, Field;

du Bois, Wood. These are but three instances out of a hundred that could be named. Who would ever suppose that Deems, Spurgeon, Dann, Blake, Dwight, Packard, Cooper, Scidmore, Hanna, Hansard, and scores of other English names were originally Dutch? Johan Winkler's book of De Nederlandsche Geslachtsnamen (Dutch Ancestral Names) shows among its thousands hundreds that are known to have been altered into other forms by immigrants to England.

Dutch Anabaptists were in Norwich by 1530. A Walloon congregation had been formed as early as 1570, so that by 1604 there must have been many English speaking children and grandchildren of these refugees from the Flemish Netherlands. In the hostile writings of this era, the "Brownists" and "Anabaptists" were usually identified as fraternal sects.

John Robinson would gladly have remained in Norwich, but persecutions and imprisonments which continually troubled him and his church members drove him to the northwest, where he soon found that the catchpoll officers and minions of the bishops were just as ready there to do their abominable work as in Norwich.

Elizabeth died in 1603, and the son of Mary Queen of Scots, James VI. of Scotland, became King James I. of England. On his way to London he passed through Scrooby, and it is possible that Brewster saw his future persecutor, and may even have served him with refreshments at the inn. One county sheriff, of Nottingham, met the king, and the other, of York, took leave of the king, at Bawtry. He slept at Worksop, lunched near Blyth, and hunted in Sherwood Forest. He showed what kind of a ruler he was going to be by having a man hanged at Nottingham without trial, which was royal lynch law. From London he wrote to the York prelate, offering to buy the manor house at Scrooby. This property had been transferred by Archbishop Sandys to his oldest son Samuel, who was Brewster's landlord, and brother of Edwin, later the warm friend of the Plymouth Colony.

Whatever hopes of living peaceably under this king the Scrooby church may have cherished were blown to the winds after the Hampton Court Conference in 1604, when the edict of "conformity or exile" went forth. In 1606 the Bishop of Durham, Tobias Matthews, was made Archbishop of York. The new prelate was a great reader of "Brownist" books. He had a nose for heresy as keen as that of a bloodhound for slave tracks. So early as March, 1607, this sheriff-like bishop began the coercion of conscience.

The Separatists had not long to wait to see the bloodhound's teeth. In March, 1607, one William Blanchard, a messenger, was sent to apprehend Gervase Nevyle, who was "one of the sect of

Baroists or Brownists holding and maintaining erroneous opinions and doctrines." For such schismatical obstinacy and irreligion he was to be delivered by straight warrant "to the hands, ward and safe custody of the Keeper of His Majesty's Castle of York." The accused appeared and made answer, March 22. It is quite probable that this Gervase Nevyle was kinsman to the writer's ancestors, the Eyres. The entry is in these words, "Office against Jervase Nevyle of Scrobie dio: Ebor." (diocese of York). The names of the informers who demanded that Richard Jackson and William Brewster, of Scrooby, gentlemen charged with Brownism, and later for not appearing "upon lawful summons at the collegiate church of Southwell," are also given. In the first hunt the seekers were unable to find their game, probably because the men were at that hour in the jail at Boston. The second attempt failed likewise, for they were probably then in Holland. The warrants issued for the arrest of Brewster are dated September 15 and December 1, 1607. A "very dangerous schismatical Separatist, Brownist and irreligious subject" is the bishop's description of each gentleman.

Under such a "Defender of the Faith" and such "shepherds of the flock," the Scrooby Separatists turned Pilgrims, and began their wandering life, changing often their skies, but never their steadfast mind. How they fled from their native land, after arrest, robbery, and imprisonment in the autumn of 1607, at Boston, and capture and separation in the springtime of 1608. between Grimsby and Hull, is a familiar narra tive which the limits of our space forbid retelling. "At sundry times and in divers manners" they left their first home, England, and reached their second home, the United States of the Netherlands.

CHAPTER VII

"INTO A NEW WORLD" — AMSTERDAM

When the Dutch sailor says that "Amsterdam is built on herring bones," he tells a "fish story" that is true. Its name pictures the dam on the Amstel River, at the side of which in the thirteenth century clustered fishermen's huts under the shadow of the feudal castle. In Dutch history the use of the word "dam" in the end of a name marks the transition from the power of the feudal lords to that of the burghers in the cities. No Dutch town whose name ends in "dam" is older than the twelfth century, after which charters and municipal rights, wrested or bought from the barons and castle lords, ushered in the era of industry and civic freedom. The fishing-village on the Amstel became a town, and then a city.

After Antwerp had, in 1585, been captured by the Spaniards, and turned over to the Jesuits, it ceased to be the home of freedom. Amsterdam then became the refuge of the oppressed of every clime. Here, in 1593, as naturally as the compass needle trembles toward the pole, moved those Londoners who, for having applied democracy to church polity, had been hunted out of their native land. There was then no waterway direct from Amsterdam to the German Ocean, nor was the North Holland canal from the Helder yet cut. All vessels had to go round by Texel Island, and into the Zuyder Zee.

We hear of parties of these English refugees at Kampen, the city now so famous for its tobacco and theology, and at Naarden, the scene of the awful Spanish massacre of 1572. Being without money or food, these stranded folk had to be helped by the town authorities; but finally getting into Amsterdam, very poor and miserably rent, divided, and scattered, they formed the "Ancient English Church" of which Henry Ainsworth was teacher. At first they received some assistance from friends in London and Middelburg. By 1607 their affairs had vastly improved. When Robinson arrived, there were no fewer than seven religious communities of English-speaking people in the great Dutch city.

One of these, the Scottish Presbyterian church, formed in 1607, remains until this day, having its place of worship off the Kalver Straat in the Beguynhof, or Court of the Beguyn Nuns. In this old edifice, once the cloister chapel of the "cell-sisters," the writer preached June 30, 1895. From the first, this Presbyterian church was connected with the State Establishment, and therefore was given an edifice by the city magistrates, while the Separatists had to find a place of worship, and pay their own rent; yet so also did the Jews, Catholics, Lutherans, Anabaptists, and other worshipers of God.

Because of their tolerance, the Dutch republicans were made the butt and byword of the English politicians and of every royal persecutor of Europe, but they cared for these as little as Americans care to-day for like gibes. They valued freedom as life itself.

It was a wonderful country—this land where conscience was free—to these people who had come from the interior rustic villages in the backward and thinly populated parts of northern England. As Bradford says, "It seemed they were come into a new world. They saw many goodly and fortified cities strongly walled and guarded with troops of armed men. Also they heard a strange and uncouth language, and beheld the different manners and customs of the people with their strange fashions and attires." It is more than probable that during the whole eleven years of their sojourn in the republic these Puritans wore what to the natives seemed a curious garb. Their English speech was "broken Dutch" to the Hollanders.

Amsterdam was already one of the world's great markets, one of its handsomest and richest cities, and was destined during the seventeenth century to excel all. It had a bank, which was then a new thing in northern Europe, nothing like it being known in England, where the rates of interest on money loaned were enormous. The city on the Amstel had mightily enlarged since the beginning of the war of independence against the Spaniards. Even in 1609 the large canals, new waterways, newly reclaimed land, and building lots, were none too ample for the increase of the population.

The first business of the newcomers was to find employment, and this they did at various occupations. It is very probable that most of them lived in that part of the city where rents and houses were cheap, as for instance around the Binnen-Amstel near the Baker Straat; that is, inside the Amstel River near Baker Street. Not far away was the street of dyehouses, on what is now the Groenen-burg, or the green thoroughfare anciently lying along the wall of the burg or castle.

A building in which some of these English folk worshiped is in a place still called, as a Dutch woman on the spot told me, "Brownisten gang," or Brownists' Alley, — the word "gang" being the same as in Robert Burns's line, "gang aft agley," or in "gangway." To-day, if one visits this place, starting from the centre of the city, say the Doelen Straat, he goes north along the Kloveniers Burgwal (that is, by the old archery-path to the Culverineers' castle wall) down to the New Market. This is an open space, at the south end of which is one of the old walled city's massive gate-houses with imposing conical towers. To the left he will notice one street called Blood Street, and another Barnde-Steeg, meaning the place of the burned. Here, between 1522 and 1578, the Anabaptists and Protestants were either beheaded or burned. Turning to the left, down one of these streets, and to the right into a narrow alley, we find at the end an uninviting-looking building, several stories high, and having walls three or four feet thick, which is now used as a tenement house. In the fourteenth century this was a convent or house of the cell-sisters. At the top of the first flight of steps there is a large low-ceiled room in which the English refugees, and probably John Robinson's company, worshiped in 1609.

Amsterdam did not come under the control of magistrates of the Reformed faith until 1578. During Alva's reign of terror, the blood of the beheaded flowed and the ashes of the burned martyrs were cast into the canals on either side of Blood Street, or of the Alley of the Burned, and were borne down into the great haven, past that famous old round tower, which then, as well as now, was occupied by the harbor-master. Even in Pilgrim days it was called the Weepers' or Shriekers' Tower, because here ships began their voyage to distant lands in the orient, America, or at the poles. The shrieks and the cries of weeping relatives mingled with the words of farewell.

From this very place, only a few days before Robinson's company arrived, their own fellow-countryman, Henry Hudson, (or in Irvingese, "Hendrik" Hudson) had sailed away. Hudson was a friend of Captain John Smith, who had just named Plymouth and sent to his fellow explorer charts of the Massachusetts coast. With his first mate, Robert Juet, Hudson sailed in the Half Moon, both his ship and crew being Dutch, to seek the northeast passage to China. Failing in this, he tried to reach the Asian gold lands by the northwest passage. He did not give up until he had entered the Hudson River and gone up to the latitude of Albany and Troy. Even then he hoped to find the waterway to Asia, but the shallowness of the stream flowing from the Adirondacks compelled him to turn back. Before Robinson and his company had left Amsterdam, the Half Moon and her Dutch crew were back again in the Amstel haven, though the grasping government of King James detained Hudson at Plymouth and did not quite give up the idea of laying claim to the lands of his discovery, because, forsooth, he was an Englishman. New England, the future home of the Pilgrims, and New Netherland, in which they intended to settle, received their names on the same day. The future "empire region" of the United States discovered by

Henry Hudson lay between New France and Virginia; and the name New Netherland, in the singular, was the symbol of the union of States in one federal republic.

For a little while the church under Smyth and that under Johnson lived in union. Then, Smyth's congregation split and quarreled; first on the subject of using translations of Scripture instead of the original, and then on the subject of the form of baptism. The other English church had its troubles because Johnson, who was aristocratic in his tastes, became more and more a Presbyterian, believing in the government of the church by elders; while Ainsworth held to the strict New Testament idea of democracy. Robinson sided warmly with Ainsworth and held to the simple democracy of the primitive Christian church.

Other troubles, not wholly ecclesiastical, in the congregation which the Scrooby folk had joined, were largely on account of feminine fashions. This was an epoch of gorgeous clothes and extravagant fashions among all classes. By a natural reaction, the protest of reformers also was great. As Cæsar had his Brutus, so Mrs. Johnson, the wife of the Rev. Francis Johnson, had her brother-in-law, who threatened to kill her reputation. This puritanical critic, having had a prolonged quarrel with his sister-in-law in London, reopened the discussion in Amsterdam. He accused her of wearing "apparel unreformed," meaning especially gay hats and jauntily trimmed dresses. On the other hand, several of the brethren believed the brother-in-law had "a crackt brain." Further particulars of offense,—spicy and comical they seem now,—and duly fortified by scriptural passages, were charged against Mrs. Johnson. One fault was that she "laid in bed on the Lord's day till 9 o'clock and hindered the exercise of the Word," the accuser supporting this last charge with four Scripture passages: Ps. cxix.; Is. lviii. 13; Ezek. xx. 12; and Acts xx. 7.

Matters were afterwards somewhat improved, and a truce followed for a few months, until the pastor's wife was so indiscreet as to buy a velvet hood, such as none but the richest, finest, and proudest ladies sought to use. This was to the brother-in-law as a red rag shaken at a bull. After much striving and wrestling of conscience about performing his duty, he wrote her a long letter which he concluded by expressing a fear lest "such attire will open the adversary's mouth, disconfute the ungodly, discredit the gospel and dishonor God."

Alternate peace and storm followed; but at all the meetings and conferences the main topic of the accuser's conversation was the pastor's wife. It came to pass that the venerable father of the husband and the brother-in-law came over from England to heal the difficulty, with the result that both father and brother-in-law were put out of the church. The final handling of the matter lasted through twelve weeks. After this excommunication the controversy of years was closed, and a short season of peace came to the church of which Johnson was pastor.

This is the sensible comment of William Bradford on this whole affair. "She (Mrs. Francis Johnson) was a young widow . . . and was a godly woman . . . Because she wore such apparel as she had formerly been used to, which were neither excessive nor immodest, for their chiefest exceptions were against her wearing of some whalebone in the bodice and sleeves of her gown, corked shoes and other such like things as the citizens of her rank then used to wear. And although for offence sake, she and he were willing to reform the fashions of them so far as might be without spoiling of their garments, yet it would not content them except they came full up to their size." Bradford then goes on to show how rigid were the notions of some Puritans even on the subject of starch.

The late Dr. Henry Martin Dexter, who, with Professor de Hoop Scheffer, has most fully studied the history of these English people in the Dutch metropolis, has given the details of what he calls "The Old Clothes Controversy" and has recovered the names of over four hundred and fifty free churchmen.

Another and a far more serious controversy broke out on the question of church polity, when Smyth came under the influence of the "Waterlander" Mennonites and the Arminians, and became a Baptist. Ainsworth and his friends seceded from Johnson and his adherents, and there was every prospect of a long continuance of unpleasantness. This decided Robinson and his company to leave the Amstel and find a home on the Rhine. Next to Amsterdam, the richest and most important city of Holland was Leyden, which was within easy reach by canal. Here all were likely to gain a livelihood, for the cloth and woolen industries of this city were famous. The great university, excellent schools, and large printing-offices attracted the lettered men of the company, who had found that Holland was a wonderful place for cheap books and first-rate education, from the free public schools to the renowned universities of the republic, two of which, Leyden and Franeker, were then in their bloom.

It is not difficult to picture this city on the Rhine in A. D. 1600, for few places on this planet have richer antiquities, archives, and memories in art. Jan Orlers, who was burgomaster of the municipality, has given in his oft-reprinted book full details of its history and administration, so that we know the important facts and hundreds of names of local officers, those from 1609 to 1625 being of most interest to Americans.

The application of Robinson, in behalf of himself and about one hundred other persons, for permission to come and reside in Leyden may still be read in the Court Day Book among the municipal archives, under the date of February 12, 1609, with the indorsed reply that "the coming of the Memorialists will be agreeable and welcome."

So it came to pass that in Leyden City in Holland, as well as in Leyden Street in America, the first sound heard from strangers who were natives of the asylum-lands of these Pilgrim exiles was the word "welcome," which they would have been so glad to hear in their home-land, but for which they had listened in vain.

Though the story of "the ancient church" in Amsterdam is a sad one, disclosing disagreeable traits of character, yet after all it is no different from that of struggling man in every age and country. The controversies, the manifestations of human infirmity, and the questions at issue were not different or any worse than those which have repeatedly occupied and vexed larger organizations and more famous assemblies. No theory of faith or system of church government can suppress or eliminate human nature. In what vital respect the discussions of convocations and synods about surplices and cassocks, gowns and vestments, candles and credence-stools, or the disputes about mysteries and dogmas, either in past centuries or in this generation, differ from those among the Separatists at Amsterdam in 1609, cannot be easily discerned.

Those Christians who were nicknamed "Brownists" maintained a church or churches in Amsterdam until 1701, though before that time most of them had united with the Dutch Baptists, Mennonites, or Friends, or had entered the Reformed church. Among them was the polished scholar and journalist William Sewall (1654–1720), who made an English-Dutch dictionary, and wrote a "History of the Quakers."

Music was cultivated by the Separatists. As early as 1562, the English hymns they sang had been put into metre and set to notes. In 1612 Henry Ainsworth published in Amsterdam "The Book of Psalmes, Englished both in Prose and Metre," which had thirty-nine separate tunes in it. For eighty years this book was part of the daily spiritual food of the Pilgrims on both sides of the Atlantic. Ainsworth, known all over Europe as a leading Hebrew scholar, whose annotations have helped even the makers of the Revised Version of 1885, was so poor a poet, and his verses were so uncouth, that the Continental scholars at first imagined there must be two Ainsworths. In trying to unravel the mystery, some of them got badly tangled up in their own higher criticism. More than one half of Ainsworth's tunes show their Netherlandish environment.

CHAPTER VIII

"A FAIR AND BEAUTIFUL CITY" — LEYDEN

AMSTERDAM in 1609 was only about one third of its present size. The great triple line of "grachts" which, like semi-circles, inclose the old and form part of the crescent city had not then been dug, nor were the inclosed spaces built upon, though this work of enlargement was carried out in the seventeenth century. The Dutch make a difference between a "gracht" and a canal. The former is one of the city moats or waterways. A canal is a longer water passage, generally between two cities, and is a highway for travel. "Gracht" is the more common word for a waterway within or near the city walls, and "canal" is used to designate a waterway from one place to another. The Pilgrims loaded their boats in a "gracht." They traveled by "canal" to Leyden.

We can imagine the little flotilla freighted with household goods and crowded with plainly and soberly dressed English people, conspicuous among whom was the dignified John Robinson. In clerical garb, and wearing a cap which looked exactly like a watermelon cut in half, with perhaps a little band of lace around the bottom, and wearing also a ruff around his neck, he would be easily recognized. Brewster, the man in middle life, being forty-two years old, and Bradford, the young bachelor of nineteen, would perhaps be prominent. The women and children would enjoy the outing in the lovely springtime, as they passed through the garden region of Europe, where even at that early time the tulips were gorgeous and the other cultivated flowers magnificent. Where now, however, are square miles of bloom and color or rich pastures dotted with cows, was then a colossal checker-board of green with squares of white, for there were acres of linen bleaching on the sward. Chlorine was not then isolated or its virtues recognized, but some qualities in the water of the Spaarn River and the skill of the bleachers, who deftly handled their wooden shovels as sprinklers, made Haarlem linen famous throughout the world.

The journey would be along the Haarlem Canal from the city until they got into the Haarlemmer meer or lake, on which naval battles between the Dutch and Spaniard had been fought. During the siege of Leyden, relief had been sent by boats in summer, and on sledges over the ice in winter, to the garrison, for the water washed the walls of both cities. The lake no longer exists, but in its place is an area of gorgeously blooming gardens, the richest bulb-lands in Holland, with villages, farms, hedges, and highways over which one rides in the steam tram. In our century, after many years of pumping by wind and steam mills, the bottom of the lake has been made visible and useful. A whole museum of curiosities, consisting of anchors, ship timber, and ship iron, relics of human beings and accoutrements of soldiers and sailors, came to light as the waters lowered.

With the fields so green, the mild-eyed cows grazing everywhere, the birds in immense numbers flitting about, it must have been an enjoyable trip both to the parents and to the children, who would note many things and clap their hands in glee over what adults might ignore. While traversing the lake and the green fields of South Holland, they saw that the great flat landscape was everywhere dominated by the church spire. In the distance, on their left, were the shining waters of the Zuyder Zee. On the right rose the great sand hills, or dunes, which form Holland's wall of defense against the ocean. This pretty country, not so very different in those days from the flat lands, marshy fens, and water-courses of Nottingham and Lincoln, would be in view all day. After the walls and great church spire of Haarlem had been left far behind, they would, probably late in the afternoon, come within sight of the turreted gates and walls of Leyden, gay with the orange, white, and blue flag of the federal republic. They would see the great church of St. Peter, "as an elephant stands among common cattle," under the shadow of which was to be their home, the roof of St. Pancras, the glorious bulb spire of the State House, from which bells sounded out sweet chimes, and the Burg, the central landmark and the highest mass of land within the city.

While on the lake they were in the open, but when nearing Leyden they turned aside into smaller and narrowing bits of water, each having its own name, until they came to the Rhine, which flows through and incloses Leyden. At the Zijl Poort, or Canal Gate, they would be challenged by the guard. When it was found that their papers were all right, they would be admitted. Then they would be allowed to take up their quarters, which probably they had already selected, in the northwestern part of the city on and near St. Ursula Street. It is very likely that some of the company from Amsterdam had already found employment and established their quarters in "the northern Venice," and that they were present to welcome the newcomers. Yet even while the little company waited in the canal outside, they could see, besides the many windmills, the spires of the halls of the guilds, in which silk, fustian, and veils were finished, approved, stamped, and sold. Leyden was a great emporium for the manufacture of all kinds of woven goods; and next to finding peace and quiet to serve God, the idea of these Pilgrims on their second journey was to get work, that they might have food and the comforts of life.

Leyden had flourished and grown up largely through the woolen manufactures. The first canal ever cut and embanked for the making of a dam was that wherein the wool-men washed their fleeces. The earliest streets took their names from the industries of those who dealt or wrought in wool,—clipping, washing, combing, carding, weaving, and finishing it. When the Pilgrims arrived, there were no large factories with machinery as there are now, but there were hundreds of houses devoted to the washing, cleaning, dyeing, carding, combing, weaving, and all the other occupations connected with the working of wool and the manufacturing of cloth. These are represented in English by the names of occupations, families, and places, such as Webb, Webber, Webster, Weaver, Blake, Blakeslee, Dyer, Spinner, Burrell, Fuller; and, in combination, Washington, Fullerton, and hundreds of others; and in Dutch by even older forms of slightly different spelling and pronunciation. These names, which are common among us to-day, show the honest trades of our forefathers. In the detailed lists of the prominent directors and overseers of the Fustian, Cloth, Bay, and Serge Halls given by Jan Orlers, we read the names of the employers of the Pilgrim fathers. In those days the only way to make a living within a walled city was by some handicraft. If these English folk had gone out into the country to work on farms, they would have been compelled to scatter, whereas their vital need and great purpose required them to keep together.

Bradford says that they put their hands to such trades and employments as they best could, and that many of them became baize and serge weavers, others wool-carders, spinners, wool-combers, hat-makers, rope-makers, twine-twisters, masons and carpenters, block-makers, cabinet-makers, stocking-weavers, brewers, bakers, tailors, and pipe-makers. The old Dutch books on "Bezigheiden," or occupations, with their spirited woodcuts drawn from life, show exactly how the laborers, mechanics, and professional men dressed, lived, and worked in this industrial era. The industrial situation was then just as I have seen it in Japan, — the finest and costliest products of the bookbinders, potters, lapidaries, weavers, and metal-workers were wrought in small shops, the vats, the wheels, the furnaces, or the looms being usually in the owner's or worker's own dwelling. Even in printing and publishing, the typesetter or compositor often worked in his own house and carried his forms, when filled, to the pressman to have his sheets printed.

Leyden was not so large then as some people think it was, that is, with "one hundred thousand" people, — which it almost certainly never had. To-day the city has about forty thousand inhabitants, and is still noted for its blankets, woolen goods, and various other manufactures, as the catalogue of the great exhibition of Leyden products held in 1889 shows. Indeed, as the old tax lists prove, Leyden probably never had much more than fifty thousand permanent residents. No city in all the world is so rich in memorials of the Pilgrims as this "Venice of the North." Certainly none is more interesting to the American of catholic appreciation and unsectional tastes, who knows how to find his way around and how to get at the records, which bear witness to the loves, the industries, the troubles, and the triumphs of the Pilgrims.

Leyden gets its name from the old Celtic word "Lugdun," which means the looking place, or outlook, referring to the great mound or burg placed anciently at the junction of the two branches of the Rhine to command both waterways. Though lying on low land, Leyden's name and situation are like that of the hill city of Lyons in France, which has in its name the same root-word, *lug*, and this is no other than that in our word "look." Before the Romans lengthened the local term to Lugdunum, or even the Teutonic tribes had come into the land, there were human habitations here. When the helmets of the legionaries flashed in the northern sunlight and written language told of this place, it was called Lugdunum Batavorum, or the Outlook of the Batavians. What is now the Breede Straat, or Broadway, was once the Roman road laid out on the old Celtic footpath and horse track which led to the seashore.

As excavations and researches to-day show, the Romans built their fortress on the old Celtic foundation of "the Burg," in the centre of the city, and also dug the Vliet, or Fleet, which is still part of the water system of Leyden. When, after five centuries of occupation, the Romans were driven back and out of the land, the Germanic peoples came again and once more rebuilt the fortress on top of the two lower foundations, Celtic and Roman, and began here their city on the forked Rhine. These were the "Anglo-Saxons." The Angles or Engels, from which England and the English get their name, must have lived a good while in Holland, for there are nearly fifty places in the Dutch kingdom to-day named "Engeland," or England, with associated names meaning the "English" hill, court, or landmark of some kind. The Saxons also passed through the land on their way to the British Isles. It may even be that one half of the immigrants into Britain called "Anglo-Saxons" were Frisians. The Pilgrims in sailing eastward to the older home-land were in the track of one line of their forefathers. They were reversing history, but only long enough to store up and unite their forces for a longer voyage and a third home.

It is more than probable that the educated men of the party, who had often worshiped in or lived under the shadow of St. Wilfrid's church at Scrooby, recognized the image of this saint so common in Dutch literature and sculpture, and so prominent on or in the Catholic church edifices of the Netherlands. Vlissingen takes its name from Wilfrid's water-flask or bottle, long kept there as a relic.

When the Counts of Holland, which was the name of the *holt* land or well-wooded region along the lower Rhine, built their castle at Leyden, the city became rich and famous for its markets and trade, and especially for its woolen products. Its guilds of mechanics and skilled workers were known throughout Europe. Already, in the Middle Ages, the city was noted for its splendid churches, for its hospitals, its orphan asylums, and its schools, where the poor received instruction free of charge, the schools being supported by public taxation. Jan Orlers's pages show that the most honorable and learned men in Leyden were among the directors and inspectors of these schools.

The original ancient city lay between the Rapenburg Gracht and the Rhine. In this most famous and oldest part stands the cathedral, or St. Peter's Church, dedicated in 1121 and enlarged in 1339. Its superb spire, once a landmark beheld far out at sea, fell in 1512. Running alongside and named after its belfry, there was, and still is, the Klok Steeg, or Bell Alley, in which the Pilgrims afterwards lived. Facing the Rapenburg is the nunnery building, with its beautiful grounds, which afterwards became the property of the university. On Broadway, the main thoroughfare of the city, was the City Hall, where so many of the Pilgrim youth and maidens went to declare their intentions of marriage. In this neighborhood are also the university library—in which Robinson spent many hours of enjoyment—and the present museum of antiquities. On the broad quays fronting the Rhine River and convenient to the boats were then, and still are, the six markets for timber, flowers, eels, sea-fish, vegetables, and butter. In short, this is still to the visitor the most interesting part of the city. Not a few things in American life, especially life in the Middle States, take their origin or precedent from Leyden.

In the year 1200 there was an enlargement of the city made by the addition of that portion of land between the Heeren Gracht and the Burg. Four other enlargements, the last in 1659, were made, and each was inclosed with walls and moats. It is the fourth increase, that made in 1610, which most interests us, because it was here, on the new and cheap lands, that the Pilgrims settled. In view of the Great Truce then completed, and the prospect of at least twelve years of peace and undisturbed business, the city magistrates and land speculators felt justified in laying out this new part of Leyden. This portion runs from the Heeren Gracht westward to Boerhave Street and the Plantage, or garden. On the southern side, facing the wide Vest Gracht, are the potato and the beast markets.

The very interesting building called the Lakenhal, or Cloth Hall, although not built until after the Pilgrims had left the city, is very stimulating to the imagination of the student, because on the outside are beautiful bas-reliefs showing all the various stages through which a piece of cloth, made in the days before steam machinery, passed, from the sheep's back until, as an attractively folded, wrapped, approved, and stamped package, it came into the hands of the cutter and tailor. To-day the old tubs, benches, looms, scissors, tools, stamps, and certificates are only curiosities. Steam, the child born of water and fire, has wrought a revolution in the methods of the cloth trade and the weaver's art.

Yet besides these relics of industry, there are other memorials within the edifice of a more general and fascinating nature, which touch the imagination, and in them one may read Leyden's history. Old Roman fossils and remains, curious old mediæval ornaments and tools, cannon-balls, arrow-shafts and bolts shot by the bow-gun, fragments of old catapults, dented helmets and armor, war-clubs, all kinds of tools for stabbing, cutting, and killing, besides jewelry and fashionable finery, and household furnishings, illustrate Leyden life in all its phases. More interesting than anything else are the reminders of the famous siege, especially the metal cooking-pot, duly inscribed, in which the hungry but panic-stricken Spaniards left their hodge-podge — a stew made of meat and vegetables — smoking hot in their fort, nearest the city walls, which they were obliged to evacuate before the Zealand "Water Beggars" on the night of October 2, 1573. Near by hangs a great silken banner upon which is painted the figure of the suffering Christ, captured from a vessel in the Spanish Armada. The streaming rays of glory in the nimbus over his head, long faded and still invisible to the naked eye, have come to resurrection in the photograph.

These relics of the siege and war of independence here gathered together were formerly in the City Hall, which on all public holidays was thrown open to the public. Undoubtedly the Pilgrim boys and girls looked with wonder and delight on these emblems of victory when they were new and fresh, and on the old paintings of Lucas van Leyden and Engelbrechtsze which Rembrandt studied, and which shed lustre on the city. Of the buildings older than the Cloth Hall, such as the Natural History Museum and the University Library, besides the Botanic Gardens, we have good contemporary pictures by Professor Swannenburch, who was also a school director. These engravings show many specimens of bird, beast, fish, and the curious things in the mineral, vegetable, and animal worlds, just as they were arranged in Pilgrim times. In the library we see that the readers, in high peaked hats and cloaks, stood at desks, while reading, and that the books were chained or held by rods. The inevitable pet dog is there also. This was the city of Rembrandt's boyhood. The miller's lad, who was destined to be the world's greatest master of light and shade on canvas, played in the same streets that were familiar to the Pilgrim boys and girls.

CHAPTER IX

LOVE, COURTSHIP, AND MARRIAGE

By the end of the first year, 1609, it is quite probable that all the men and older boys and girls of the Pilgrim church company who wanted to get work at various trades and occupations outside of their own homes, had been able to do so; for Leyden at this very time was in a high state of prosperity. Employment was quite easy to obtain, though perhaps only a few of Robinson's company were skilled craftsmen. Even before they arrived, there were many people from the British Isles already living in Leyden. Most of these, who were neither students nor military men, were engaged in some kind of business or manual occupation connected with the making of woolen goods. As we can see from the Dutch records, these foreigners in Holland came principally from southern and eastern England, though a few were from the western and northern counties, and some also from Scotland and Ireland. In the list of twenty-four British citizens in Leyden from 1603 to 1608, five were Scotchmen, one was an Irishman, but nearly all of them were woolen-workers. The various books in the Leyden archives which contain records of the Pilgrims are the book of burghers or citizens, the lists of those paying poll tax, the registries of deeds and securities, the university records, and the book of burials.

The greatest number of Pilgrim names is found in the Trouw, or Troth Book, and are those of persons declaring intentions of marriage, who came with their witnesses or sureties. While in Leyden, as is quite certain, the Pilgrims were in the main a happy and a healthy company, and the majority of them enjoyed life richly. So early as December 4, 1610, we find in the Trouw, or Betrothal Book, on page 162, that "William Pantes," a fustian-worker, come out of England from "Marendorf," near Dover, appeared with his witnesses, "William Bruwster, Rogier Wilson, and Eduwaert Sutwaert," to give notice of his marriage with "Wibre Hanson," a young maid out of England who appeared with three friends, "Janneken White, Anna Foller, and Maryt Bottaer."

One can easily recognize the true English form of these names in their Dutch caricatures. In later history we find that Mr. and Mrs. William Pantes did not go to America, because when their opportunity came they were probably too old. The good wife of 1610 is found in the midsummer of 1611 coming as voucher for Margaret Oldham, a maiden from England, who married

Willem Berset (William Basset), of Sandwich, the widower of Sisle Lecht (Cecil (?) Lecht). Basset, whose name is the fourth to declare intentions, was to have married "Mayke Botler" (Mary Butler), of Norwich, but "De bruid is gestorven bij het derde gebod," that is, the bride died before the third publication of the banns. However, Basset soon found a new bride, for whom Wybre Pantes vouched, and Mr. and Mrs. Basset went in due time to Plymouth.

We can imagine these little parties coming over out of Belfry Lane into the Broad Street. They go up the steps of that same City Hall which we still see, and into the room of the registry. There they give their names, which we read in the once white vellum-bound books, now yellowish with age. They are written in the best manner possible, after filtering through a Dutch ear, and reappearing in the spelling of a Dutch clerk. I confess that, in looking over the Leyden records, considerable study was required in some cases to discover the English originals, so strangely transmuted in their Dutch orthography. Yet I can assure the reader that Dutch names in England have fared equally hard. There are thousands of genuine Netherlandish names, especially in the eastern and the southern counties, and in New as well as in Old England, which in the records look, read, and sound as if pure English.

To-day thousands of people having in their

veins what they believe to be "the bluest of English blood" bear not only Dutch names in an altered form, but have plenty of Dutch ancestral blood in their arteries. Even in the Pilgrim company and Plymouth Colony the names of Dutch men and women and of the numerous French folk as well, are anglicized beyond the recognition of an ordinary Hollander, such as "Simmons" for Symonson, "Cuthbert Cuthbertson" for Godbert Godbertson, and "Mullins" for Molines, or Molineaux. Other names on the tongues of speakers of English suffered surprising changes. Bompasse was compressed into Bump, La Douce into Dewson, and de la Noye into Delano. The prefix "de" in nearly all the Netherland or French names has melted into the main word, as seen in scores of instances, such as D'Albert, D'Anvers, De Haan, De Hahm, which have become Dolbeare, Danvers or Denver, Dann, Damm or Deems, respectively.

Still further, while we may think the Dutchmen queer fellows, thus to play pranks with the already unsettled orthography of English names, we must remember that the English language, as it sounded on the tongues of these rustic folk from the back country of North England, was not precisely the same as that heard in London's West End in our day. When, again, we consider the varying values of consonants and vowels in our patchwork alphabet, — which we inherit as the cast-off garments which Hebrews, Phœnicians, Greeks, and Romans have used before us, — there is no mystery about the grotesque forms in the Leyden and Amsterdam records. In many cases it is not at all certain that the intending brides and bridegrooms of the Pilgrim company could have written or spelled their own names even so well as did the Dutch functionaries of the goose-quill. Like numerous lords and ladies in the Europe of that day, some of the Pilgrim fathers and mothers could not write their own names, nor was this any disgrace then.

Any authorized person, civil or clerical, who has joined in marriage many score couples, native and foreign, and written out licenses or made registration of vital statistics will easily understand this. I know from experience that the correct recording of the names of shy or embarrassed young people, who have had need but rarely to pronounce their full and formal names to a stranger, is very difficult. Again, the whole matter of spelling, either in Dutch or English, is even now hardly under the domain of law. In the sixteenth century the situation was that of anarchy. In his history, Bradford spells the same word in six or seven different ways, and men more learned than he often twisted even a well-known proper name "nine ways out of shape." In most old English documents, one can discover so many varieties of cacography as a postmaster can collect in one of our American towns of Indian or classic name, such as Omaha or Romulus. Even of Ithaca — a name that has been in written language, polished speech, and classic editions during three thousand years — over twenty-five variations have been noted, and many educated people give two dotted vowels to the name of the city associated with the one-eyed Cyclops.

Nor do we imagine that the majority of young people of Belfry Lane, with slight thought for posterity and no dream of history, cared much more than a fig how the Dutchmen wrote their names. These, pronounced hastily and awkwardly, their true spelling often perhaps unknown to their owners, who rarely saw them in writing, were hard enough for a Dutch ear to catch. Of seven Pilgrim leaders, the birthplaces of only four are known, and of two only has the baptismal record been found in England. What is true of the leaders is at least equally so of the rank and file.

Coming down from the Stad-Huis, due proclamation of the banns by the city clerk would follow, exactly as I have seen them read in Holland and Friesland. The young folk would be married by civil process, and then would follow the marriage feast, with plenty of innocent gayety, jest, and mirth, despite the fact that they were genuine Puritans.

To continue the story of love and marriage, we find that on the 30th of December, 1610, John Jennings, a fustian-worker from Colchester, in England, never before married, and accompanied by Roger Williams and Edward Southworth, both of whom vouched for him, came with Elizabeth Pettenger, never before married, out of England, who had as vouchers Anna Ras and Janneken Peck. This betrothal does not seem to have ripened into marriage, for no further record of banns is given, but we find Elizabeth coming on November 20, 1613, to vouch for her sister Dorothea, who is to wed the widower Henry Crullins, of Amsterdam.

There were no more weddings apparently until April and May, 1611; but from that time forth are the registrations of no fewer than about fifty marriages, which in ten years is a pretty fair record for a church company never at any one time numbering over probably three hundred communicants. Puritanism never hindered love, but purified it. The Song of Songs declares that love is a fire of God. These folk from Merrie England no doubt had many pleasant though modest wedding festivals.

Not all the Separatists lived on the Rhine. We find the future governor, William Bradford, in Amsterdam November 9, 1613. He has come to declare his intentions to wed Dorothy May, who signs herself "Dority," thus leaving on the city records her only known sign-manual. Theirs is "a tale of two cities." Like Moses, she was destined to see a promised land, yet not enter it, for after seven years of married life she was drowned from the Mayflower off Cape Cod. Young men from Leyden went to the cities on the Amstel and Rotte to marry English or Dutch girls. Others came from various states of the republic to the city of St. Peter's Keys on the Rhine to do their courting, to woo, and to win. The rosy-cheeked lads and lassies from England did not confine themselves to their own nation, but married freely among the men and maids of the land.

Indeed, one of the causes which finally decided the leaders to cross the sea was the fact that, as a company, they were being gradually merged into the Dutch people, through marriage of their sons and daughters, as well as by the enlistment of the young men in the Dutch army, navy, and mercantile marine. There was danger of their tiny ark being swamped in the Dutch ocean.

To resume our list, we find that Degory Priest had for his witnesses William Leslie and Samuel Fuller. Here are the names of Isaac Allerton and Edward Southworth, of Bridget Robinson and Sarah Priest, of Thomas Morton and Alexander Carpenter, appearing as witnesses. Again, Samuel Fuller appears as a widower. Jacob Mekancke, who is a "hand-shoe" or glove maker from Scotland, marries an English maid. By November 20, 1613, we find that Henry Collins, a bombazine-maker from England, living in Amsterdam, has come down to Leyden to get married. He brings to the City Hall as his voucher the Leyden lover who has himself been wooing in the metropolis. This is William Bradford, who becomes a husband ten days later. It is written in Leyden that on the 8th of November, 1613, William "Kadfort," a fustian-worker, "van Oosterfeldt in Englandt," has given notice of his engagement to "Dorothea May, van Witzbuts, in Engelandt." The two were made one in the northern city on the 30th of November. It is quite evident that on that day either the Dutch clerk must have been an old fellow who could not hear very well, or Bradford did not speak up clearly, for after the absurd "Kadfort" the Dutchman has put in parentheses, "Badfort or Hadfort." Yet this is none other than our first American historian, William Bradford, who perhaps did not roll his *r* like the later dwellers in the land of the east wind. Dorothy May was from Wisbeach, in Lincolnshire, which is very rich in Dutch names and blood, and after her name (which was a common Dutch as well as English one, as we see in Cape May, for example) the clerk wrote, "has not appeared but has delivered an attestation." In the next notice of banns and marriage, Bradford appears with Moses

Fletcher, widower of Maria Evans, who is going to marry Sarah Dinbay, the widow of William Dinbay.

Most of the males who thus far had come to get married were makers of baize or serge or gloves or shoes, but on September 5, 1614, we meet on the written page with one who is a "boy," "Jehan Jene" (John Jenney) from Norwich, England, living at Rotterdam, and working in a brewery, who has found in Leyden her who in his eyes is the fairest among women, "Sara Kaire" (Sarah Carey), a maid from "Moucksoom." On the 22d of May, 1615, Roger Chandler, whose name is spelled (and from a Dutch point of view most properly) Kandelaer, from Colchester, marries a maid Isabel from Canterbury; which, as it stands on the records, is "Cantelberch." We see how the Dutch "burg" becomes in English "bury," "borough," "burgh," or "burg," and how the *k* in "kerk" or "Kandelaer" becomes *ch*, as in "church" and "Chandler."

In July, 1615, Samuel Butler, whose name appears as Boetlaer, and who was a "koopman" (in English cheap-man or chapman, meaning a merchant, while a partner is a coop-mate), brings for his vouchers Samuel Fuller, the doctor, and William Jepson, the carpenter, of whom we shall hear again. When Edmond Jesep (or Jepson, as the Dutch clerk adds), a bombazine-worker, comes to declare his love for Abigail Hunt, who is an unmarried girl from France, but who came from England, the clerk adds that he lives in the Greenport over the Belfry.

There was a good deal of known Dutch blood infused into the Leyden and Plymouth company, before all the immigrant ships from Delfshaven had crossed the Atlantic. The names of "Nelken Kaerlil," a young maid "out of Holland in England," with "Anneke Ras," her sister, may not have been Dutch; but Elizabeth Willincks, who wedded Roger Wilson, had a Dutch name. On the 17th of April, 1616, we find that Robert Lamkin appeared with his intending brother-in-law, as his only witness or voucher, to marry Miss Jacob Mijntje Jucosar de Graef, who is a fair maid of Leyden. She bears a family name famous in science and politics. The physician who discovered the Graafian vesicle, and the governor of the West India Island of St. Eustatius, who fired the first salute to the American flag of thirteen stripes, without stars, — to mention no others, — bore that name. On May 13, 1616, Mr. Heraut Wilson, the pump-maker, entered the City Hall, in company with William Jepson and John Carver, to marry Elizabeth Claes, from "Sermuyde," of England, whose vouchers were Sarah Minther and Dorothy Bradford, wife of William, or so at least do we understand the Dutch of "Derreke Bretfort."

Other spellings of English names are sufficiently amusing. Zachariah Burr becomes "Sacarius Boore," Cushman becomes "Coetsman," the said Robert Cushman declaring his intentions, 19th of May, 1617, and marrying, on the 3d of June, Mary Singleton, whose name appears as "Chingelton."

Most naturally the Dutch clerks in spelling names reverted, as it were, from Lowest Dutch or English, to Platt, or Middle Dutch, which is Hollandish, German being High Dutch. Hence, we find not only Osterfeldt for Austerfield, but Stephen Butterfield's name as Butterfelt. He was a silk-worker.

Up to the year 1617 the trades of the young men marrying, are, in monotonous succession, those connected with the products of the sheep, but thereafter we find men who had every day to handle black pads and type, and wash printer's ink off their fingers. There was a good deal of typesetting and presswork done in Leyden, where stood the great Elzevir house, whose books are famous all over the world, and whose printing is in quality hardly excelled to-day.

It is quite probable that some of the journeymen printers in the Pilgrim company were at work in this establishment. Among other books on the press in 1617 was the folio volume of Professor Ubbo Emmius of Groningen, who tells us so minutely about local government in the towns of democratic Friesland. There, with prayer, ballot-box, and a written ballot, magistrates were chosen. Lands were divided and held in common, and things were done generally in very much the same way that the Pilgrim Fathers afterward set them going in New Plymouth.

Wherever printers go Cupid follows. We read, in the first mention of a printer among the Pilgrims, that on the 28th of July, 1617, "Jan Reynouts" (John Reynolds), who is a young "gesel" from London, is going to marry Prudence Grindon, a young daughter and maid from England, whose avouching companions are Maria Brewster and Mary Allerton. Passing over other names, we come to another printer, Edward Winslow, a young man from London who, on April 27, 1618, declared his intentions of marrying Elizabeth Barker, which he did on the 17th of May, 1618, her place of origin being "Chatsum;" but whether this be meant for Chester or for Cadzand, we cannot tell. The next record is that of Samuel Lee, a hat-maker. The next is a brick-maker, Roger Simons, who hails from Sarum, but dwells in Amsterdam. He has come down to Leyden to marry Sarah Minther, the widow of William Minther, she appearing with her father and mother as vouchers. Again, John Smith, a widower, marries "Elsgen Knets."

In September, 1619, we find that John Codmore, a widower, whose trade is that of linen-weaver, is to marry the maid Sarah Hooper.

Here, as in so many other places, we learn that certain men and women of the church company were more frequently at the City Hall acting as match-makers, — using the word in a good sense, — or witnesses, than others. This may have been not only because of their respectability, character, and station, but also, as is very probable, because of their geniality and willingness to help young people put their necks into the matrimonial yoke. The last record that we find, before the first company or advanced guard of the young and strong went off in the Speedwell to England, is of Leonard Dunster, a silk-worker. As the Dutch record tells us, he came with his prospective father-in-law, while his betrothed, "Maycken Bruynes," a young maid from Colchester, England, is accompanied by "Mayken Sullenders," her mother, who may have been twice a widow, for evidently there is a step-parent in the case.

Two or three days after the Mayflower company had stepped ashore at Plymouth, record was made of Stephen Tracy, who was evidently, as we judge from the name, like Samuel Terry, Hester Cooke, the Mullins family, Edward Burcher, Anthony Dix, Mrs. Tracy, and others, of Huguenot, or Walloon, birth or descent. Tracy was the last of the forefathers who went to America who can be traced on the list at the City Hall. He married "Tryfoce [Triphosa] Le——." Evidently the Dutch clerk did not catch the other name, but what odds? Certainly there was no hindrance, for they were married on January 2, 1621. Evidently she also was a Walloon, as the prefix "Le" shows. Still further in the City Hall list down to 1630, we meet with over a score of records of the betrothal and marriage of British wool-combers and hat-makers, and workers in serge, baize, cloth, and bombazine, — for Laud was impoverishing England to enrich Holland, driving out the Nonconformists, — but on the 10th of May, 1629, we find "John Grynwith," who was a student in theology and probably the same as John Grinwodus (Greenwood), of the Leyden University entrance record of July 9, 1625. After courtship and graduation, he returned to marry Bridget Robinson, daughter of the pastor, who came with her mother as a witness. Bridget was then a common name among English women. Cromwell addressed not a few of his letters to his wife, "Dear Biddy."

We find that our friend "Jan Reynouts," the printer, having become a widower, went up to Amsterdam, where he found a new wife, Persis Baly, who was living by the Beurse (Bourse) or Exchange at Amsterdam. The last of the records is that of Thomas Philips, a serge-worker from Norwich, who married Susannah Siers, from Sandwich, England, on July 25, 1630. All these dates, we must remember, were in the new, or modern style, while

English dates of that period were like those of Russia in our times, — ten days beyond the rest of the civilized world. The Dutch, though stern Protestants, did not hesitate to be in the van of science even though the calendar had been made by the Pope.

This church company of men and women, who, because of the union of politics and religion, had been uprooted from their homes and driven from their native land, arrived in a country where, in all its history of many centuries, the fires of man's master passions were never hotter. The struggle between caste, privilege, and monarchy in religion, led by Spain on the one hand, and democracy in state and church, led by Holland and Zealand on the other, had been going on for forty years. Because in substance victory had been already won, the English refugees had rest and time for growth. Among themselves the great dominating, overmastering, organizing, and unifying idea was that of religion, but politics were not forgotten. They hoped to see a purified church, and they prepared also to establish "the republic of God." Yet as we have seen, the business of love went on industriously, and just so soon as bread was provided, there were marriages many and in continuance.

Necessarily the Leyden records preserve only a portion of the names of those who were married out of the church company in Belfry Lane.

The names of those daughters and sons who went elsewhere in the republic than to Rotterdam and Amsterdam to wed Dutch, English, or French yoke-fellows, as well as the names of the young men who enlisted in the Dutch army and navy to fight the Spaniards, or who went on voyages of discovery, exploration, or trade will probably never come into the realm of the known. Still less are we likely to recover the names of those who, not liking the strict ways of the Leyden Pilgrims, went back to England, or, settling among the Dutch, lived what seemed to them more reasonable and pleasant lives. In Amsterdam, as Dr. Scheffer has found, there were one hundred and eighteen marriages among these English exiles from twenty-nine counties, between 1598 and 1617.

One of these Englishmen in the Netherlands, named John Starter, though we are not certain that he was a Separatist, became a famous poet and singer in Friesland. He lived a gay and luxurious life, and has left behind him many sweet and stirring songs and amorous and humorous poems in elegant Dutch, thus making income and fame. His works are still reprinted in fine editions.

There do not, so far as we can see, appear to have been many intermarriages of these plain English Separatists, most of them mechanics and country people, with the other British people in the church next door to them, under the pastorate of the Rev. Robert Durie, whose salary was paid by the city of Leyden, or with the other English churches, of which eight or ten of the whole number of twenty-six or thirty known in the seventeenth century, were then in the Netherlands before 1620. The Separatists made unions for life more commonly with the Walloons and Dutch than with the English or Scottish people of the state churches of Great Britain.

While the Pilgrims were in Holland, the Book of Common Prayer was translated into Dutch. There were many marriages of English and Scottish soldiers with Dutch women.

Three Pilgrim men were especially interested in local and practical politics. They were William Bradford, Isaac Allerton, and Degory Priest. The future governor was the first to avail himself of the privileges of citizenship in Leyden, his registration as freeman having been made March 30, 1612, Roger Wilson and William Lysle being his securities. Roger Wilson did not come to America, but seems to have been otherwise a prominent man in the company, for on February 7, 1614, he became security for Isaac Allerton, and on November 16, 1615, for Degory Priest, the hatter. These men would thus, by becoming citizens of Leyden, and personally and practically enjoying its privileges, learn the working of municipal government and ward organization, and be interested in the movements of politics in a municipal and federal republic.

Political procedure in the Low Countries was considerably different from that in England; and though republicanism was then in a very imperfect condition, yet it was in spirit and often in form like that of the later government in the United States of America. With the living example of a federal republic before them, and in a country which counted as one of its States Friesland, where the tastes and methods of the people were of the most democratic kind, the Pilgrims could not but learn much that fitted them to be builders of a new commonwealth. In Friesland, local government was still the general rule. There the old Teutonic ideas, of the town, with the rights of pasture, woodland and water held in common, were still kept up. Instead of being comparatively dead traditions, as in England, these were working and effective. Many of these Dutch ideas have gone into the law, especially of the Middle States, notably of New York and Pennsylvania.

There was no absolute liberty at that time anywhere in Europe, yet throughout the Dutch republic there was an atmosphere of wonderful freedom of speech and of the press, and in the Dutch churches there was a democracy which compelled the more aristocratic city and state governments to execute the popular will. In later centuries the American people, in the evolution of their destiny and confronted by the problems of federal politics, borrowed ideas, laws, constitutional principles, and even pet phrases, approved standard methods, and party names, from the republic in which the Pilgrims found asylum and education.

CHAPTER X

WORK AND PLAY IN LEYDEN

HOW many children were born in the Leyden church company between 1610 and 1620? How many lived and grew up among Dutch playmates and learned their speech? It is very probable that not a few of the Pilgrim children went to the Dutch free public schools, where they acquired the rudiments of education in the sister language which is nearest to English. We may judge that at least twenty children came first to Leyden in 1610, and that about one hundred were born or lived a longer or shorter space in Holland and became familiar with Dutch things and ideas.

Leyden, from the early Middle Ages, as her archives still show, had a noble story of popular, as well as of special education. Besides the Dutch public schools, there was also one for the Walloons in Leyden. From these records, the contemporaneous paintings, and the little book entitled "A Peep into the Old School World," published in Leyden in 1890, when a great exhibition of the antiquities, as well as of the modern improvements in Dutch national education was held, we can form a clear idea of the comparative excellence of instruction in the elementary public schools, which were free to the poor.

A proportion of the Pilgrim company became coop-mates, — to use the old English word, — or partners with the natives, their fellow workmen. Living while at work in every-day association with Leyden people, they must have learned to think and talk in Dutch. Especially the younger and more intelligent portions must have so acquired the language as to use it fluently and well. Bradford, Winslow, and others, as we know, were able to write Dutch. In the library of the Pilgrims' own writings, there is frequent mention of "our members that understood the [Dutch] language."

No doubt this noble speech of a free people sounded, as it still does to all who first hear it and do not know it, "uncouth." The Dutch is not a dialect of German. It is a language by itself, and is one of the strongest, clearest, and best fitted to express high ideas and to resist the intrusion of foreign elements. The speech of Erasmus, Grotius and Vondel is as different from that of Luther, Goethe, and Schiller as English is different from Dutch. When the Separatists arrived in the Netherlands the Dutch language had already been cultivated and adorned by the writings of a host of poets, prose-writers, scholars, dramatists, jurists, and men of science.

It had even been made the subject of critical research, being one of the first languages in Europe to be so treated, for Killian was one of the foremost pioneers in modern linguistic science.

Scholarly English-speaking students of Dutch know that the likeness between the two languages spoken on opposite sides of the North Sea is very close, and that Dutch is especially the repository of the old and dear and hallowed words in English speech and literature. It must not be forgotten that the later British prejudices against their neighbors, which arose out of commercial jealousy and the wars of Cromwell and Stuart days, were unknown to the Pilgrims, as well as to most Englishmen before A. D. 1630.

The children, besides easily picking up a new language with far more rapidity than adults, see a thousand things which their elders do not notice. As a rule, a child's range of observation is of things not higher than the top of a yardstick. A five-year old boy notices what is close at hand or on the ground. He has keen impressions of those things primitive and basic, to which a grown person is often numb or callous. He easily becomes acquainted with animals. He likes the unconventional and natural. In Leyden the elders might wrinkle their foreheads over the future and be sad with forebodings, but the children were happy. Despite the troubles of their parents, — hardship and toil, and at times poverty, the uncertain future, the dangers from their sovereign to life, limb, and liberty, the wrestling with spiritual and social problems, — the young folk were happy, knowing as a rule nothing of the things unseen or unfelt. Leyden was at that time the heart of Holland; and since it was one of the liveliest cities in Europe, life there must have been very delightful to the boys and girls.

Beyond the walls, water-courses and flowery meadows lured them to angle or to stroll, and the seashore was only a few miles off. In winter skating, sleighing, sledding, and the merry games of the people made fun and frolic.

Inside the city, they could go up on the Burg, and, looking over the country for miles around, have pointed out to them the historic sites made famous during the siege. Their Dutch friends, who had heard it from their fathers, could tell the story. Quite probably some of the older men and women, who had once suffered almost to starvation and it may be to wounds, were glad to fight once more the battle over again. Here rose a Spanish bastion. There such a body of troops camped. In this village the Spanish commander had his headquarters. Yonder the Leyden boy, Gisbert Cornellison, in early morning waded out and found the fort of Lammen empty and the stew-pot (still kept as a precious relic) hung over the fire and full of "hutch-putch." As on a map, flat Holland lay before them.

They could see the fields which had been flooded by cutting the dikes at Delfshaven, the sluice-gates up to which the Zealand relief ships came, and the place where the sailors tossed up herring and loaves to the starving people. They would hear told many a wonderful tale and anecdote. The carrier pigeons which carried messages to and from friends outside, had been gratefully cared for and fed, and after their death were stuffed and kept as memorials. All Leyden was full of reminders, and scars, even then fresh, of the great siege, which had lasted one hundred and thirty-one days.

Most popular and interesting of all the single festivals — for the Kermiss, or universal merry-making, lasted a week — was the annual Thanksgiving Day on October 3, when all the Dutch people of the city went to church to thank God for deliverance from the enemy and for his mercies, and then returned home to eat their favorite historic dish, — a stew of meat and vegetables, Spanish hodge-podge, or hutch-putch, as they called it, — in memory of their fathers. To this dish they added dainties and rich things for joy and gladness. Thus the Pilgrims had before them a living example, which they could never forget, of an annual Thanksgiving Day to God. Like equally sacred commemorative days in America and in all the world, perhaps, the mode of celebration became after a few generations less rigidly religious. For those festivals handed down from the Roman form of Christianity the Pilgrims would have little sympathy and much antipathy; but at the holidays of Santa Claus, or St. Nicholas (which is not the same as Christmas), New Year's Day, the Maypole festivities, the Kermiss, and the local and national rejoicings there is little doubt that many of the English folk rejoiced with their Dutch fellow-Christians of the Reformed faith.

Jan Steen, born in 1626, and one of the world-renowned Leyden school of artists, has painted the joyous merriment in a Dutch home on the day of Santa Claus, or St. Nicholas. Heaps of cookies, waffles, and sugar-loaves, and baskets of toys amuse the youngest of the children. One small boy plays with his father's cane. The daughter puts hay in the shoe to show the naughty older boy that he will get only that from Santa Claus. This unlucky urchin is making such a wry face that he looks as if he had taken a pinch of snuff, but he is only crying. The windows, fireplace, curtained or closet bed, and the cozy comforts of home life are pictured with spirit. They show scenes and surroundings familiar especially to those members of the Separatist church who had social privileges above the average, and who were addressed as "Mr." and so wrote their names — a right and reservation now free to all.

The young people having that keen sense of the ludicrous, which no Puritanism can remove, and having light spirits and few cares, must have enjoyed plenty of fun. That the young quite largely, and the adults moderately, at least, saw and appreciated the ludicrous side of Dutch life, may be surely believed. From what we learn from Bradford, who showed his wit in his letters, History, and Dialogue, the old deaconess had her hands full during church hours in keeping the lively boys and girls in order. In the Dutch church the sermon always consisted of a prelude, or *exordium remotum*, and an application; while with Bible reading, psalm singing, and prayers and *two* collections, the services would be at least two hours long. In the Pilgrim house of worship the time would probably be no shorter, making it hard for juvenile flesh and blood to stand the tedium. The service in both the Dutch and the English churches was much the same, especially in length.

Many famous visitors came to this city of learned men, and the people in Bell Alley could hear a good deal of English spoken on the streets by hundreds of English people, students, soldiers, merchants, contractors, and their families. These Pilgrim folk were not lonely, except as they chose, for the sake of a high purpose and noble ideal, to make themselves so.

The number of English-speaking students was

especially great after the universities of the homeland had been closed to the people of the four nations at large in the British Isles, and became accessible only to those of the one sect patronized by the state. In the list of students we find the name of Robert Durie, the minister of the English church which met in a house on the lot next to that of the Pilgrims. He matriculated in 1610. Being fifty-five years old and married, it is evident that he and men like Robinson, who had wives and families, were what we should call special students; for connection with the university gave one a position in the society of the city which was very desirable, and of which the Pilgrim leaders took rightful advantage. On February 7, 1615, Thomas Brewer, whose name was spelled "Braber," matriculated as a student of literature. On August 26, 1615, the Rev. John Robinson, then thirty-nine years old, entered as a student of theology.

While Durie is described as the minister of "the English church," which, by the way, was largely attended by Scottish people, nothing is said about Robinson's being the pastor of a church. The reason of this seems to me to be plain. All congregations that were professedly in conformity with the general doctrines and order of the Reformed faith in Europe, — among which the Church of England, as well as of Scotland, was recognized as one, — were not only acknowledged as churches by the Dutch magistrates, but were furnished with places of worship, and the salaries of the ministers were paid in whole or in part at the cost of the city. Robinson and his people, however, no more allowed or approved the regulation of the church by the magistrates, than the Dutch recognized his company as a church, by giving him and them a church edifice or house of worship, whether they wanted it or not. Both parties left each other alone, and this beautifully and appropriately, with mutual satisfaction. Robinson's application from Amsterdam for residence in Leyden, and the freedom of the city "in carrying on their trades without being a burden in the least to any one," dated February 12, 1609, shows the independent spirit of the Pilgrims. It contains no suggestion of asking for a house of worship from the authorities. Neither Robinson nor his people ever asked for a house of worship free, or for any pecuniary assistance in religious matters, for such a proceeding would have been against their principles. They wanted only full toleration, and they got it. The university record, in Latin, states that Robinson entered by permission of the magistrates, and that he had a family.

Besides his literary and social privileges, a fellow of the university was free from patrol duty in time of war. He could buy or brew a certain amount of beer, or make wine for his private use free of excise tax. He also enjoyed freedom from arrest by authorities other than those of the university. This immunity, which the British king vainly tried to ignore, prevented extradition to any foreign country at the whim of a sovereign. Membership in the university proved a tower of defense to Brewer and Brewster, and shielded them from the clutch of James Stuart and his henchman, Laud, when these worthies were troubled by the freedom which the Dutch allowed to authors and printers.

All things considered, the Pilgrim community prospered well, for they had been in Leyden only about a year when they were able to buy, at a bargain, a lot in Bell Alley, or Belfry Lane, in the very heart of the city, and its oldest and finest part, directly opposite and parallel with St. Peter's Church, and adjoining on the rear the lot and house where the other English church worshiped. It was within almost a stone's throw of the university and the Rapenburg upon the one side, and of Broad Street, on which was the City Hall, upon the other; that is, about midway between the two. The purchasers were four men, not one of whom went to America, — John Robinson, the pastor; William Jepson, the carpenter, his brother-in-law; Randolph Tickens, a looking-glass maker, and Henry Wood. These four, as agents of the church company, bought a house and garden, paying for them eight thousand guilders, which, expressed in our money values of to-day, would be about sixteen thousand dollars. Of this sum they paid two thousand guilders down, and the remainder in easy installments during May of every year until all was paid, — "the last penny with the first."

The deed — the scene of the drawing and registry of which we can, after our visits to the City Hall, easily imagine — was dated May 5, 1611. There are some who imagine the Pilgrim Fathers to have been men directly inspired to invent institutions and customs, such, for example, as the registration of land deeds and mortgages. Such notions and statements are amusing to one who has made himself acquainted with the riches of Leyden's archives, and of those at Leeuwarden, Groningen, Zwolle, Dordrecht, and other Dutch cities. The Pilgrims saw much and improved on some things which they saw, but we Americans are debtors to the Dutch as well as to the English. The registration of deeds and mortgages and the ease of access for proof and publicity is an old story in the Netherlands, and for the seventeenth century a wonderful one.

We have also copied out from the Dutch archives a sketch of the grounds and lots as they were before the purchase, showing that the lot which they bought from Jan de La Laing was the one nearest the Commandery and Heeren Straat. At this Commandery, as being the military headquarters, Miles Standish and other English officers would no doubt frequently visit or be on duty. Here, perhaps, Standish first got acquainted with the brave men who were to be his future comrades in arms beyond sea. The lot purchased of La Laing, and one of two owned by him, was one hundred and twenty-five feet in length; and at the rear of it, just beyond a well, rose a wall inclosing the land on which stood the old chapel of the Veiled Nuns' Cloister, on the lower floor of which the English church, to which the Rev. Robert Durie preached, met for worship, while on the upper floor was the famous university library.

Here was their opportunity. They had land enough on which to build a number of small houses in which families could live, forming a settlement which would attract little public notice; for to the outward eye it was much like those numerous communities, not only of nuns and monks, but also of aged married couples, and of old men and women, which were so common in the Netherlands. Within these hofs, or courts, where we see many little houses built around the central garden or open space, a noteworthy proportion of the less active part of the inhabitants of Holland still live. There are over forty hofs in Leyden and many more in Amsterdam. Hence, we frequently find the word "hof," a memorial of origins, in Dutch family names. Thus this feature of Dutch city life fitted admirably to the Separatists' needs, and enabled them to carry out their purpose without seeming to be odd or eccentric. The Pilgrims were able to live as a genial society, having their own rules of life. "They stood on their own legs" more closely even than when at Scrooby or in Plymouth, for they were more independent. They had less alloy and adulteration in their mass than when in the wilderness.

Robinson's large "house" became their place of worship; for then, as now and in the early New Testament times, a church was not a building, but a congregation of believing Christians. Their edifice for worship, whether looking like a "church" or not, was their meeting "house." The Pilgrims willingly and gladly chose to do what the Roman Catholics and other dissenters and sects outside the state church were compelled to do, that is, to worship in a house that did not look like a "church." They were people who cared more for reality than phenomena. To them the life was more than the meat, and the body more than the raiment. Furthermore, they were familiar with such New Testament passages as Rom. 16. 5; 1 Cor. 16. 19; Col. 4. 15. It must not be forgotten that in North English parlance the word "house" meant particularly the parlor, place for conversation, or chief sitting or living room, and in this part of Robinson's dwelling was the meeting "house."

Under the direction of Jepson, who was a carpenter, there were put up no fewer than twenty-one houses, probably then built of wood, though now the little houses standing on the same lot are of brick; and so this Pilgrim place of abode made a "town" within the city. Primitive Germanic speech made a distinction between the "house" and the "home;" the former was the edifice or dwelling, while the latter was the ground within which was the house. The town was the hedge or inclosure wherein the community dwelt. To this day the Dutch word "tuin," the original of our word "town," means a garden. When a bill advertising a house and lot to be sold is posted, as the owner of the lot in Bell Alley possibly had caused to be done before Robinson purchased, the sign is "Huis en tuyn te koop," or literally, house and garden for sale.

Without holding their goods in common, the Pilgrims made a covenant with each other to bear one another's burdens. It is even possible that the whole company was accommodated inside the houses, which were arranged on two sides of the long quadrangle. When, years afterwards, they made a settlement at Plymouth, it was laid out on exactly the same model — "two rows of houses and a fair street."

These humble dwellings of the church company in Leyden were not built with all the solidity, comforts, and conveniences of the best Dutch houses, which stand on piles, are of brick well anchored with iron, and have walls tiled, papered, or tapestried, many windows furnishing abundance of light and air, spacious hearths and chimneys, sociable stoop or doorsteps, with a canopy and seats, and those handy double doors which allow ventilation and light while keeping out animal intruders. Nevertheless in the Pilgrim settlement the dwellings were doubtless made as cheery and comfortable as the means of their owners allowed. The purchasers did not get possession of their property until May 1, 1612, for the Dutch moving day was May 1. This idea having been borrowed by the founders of New Netherland, "Moving Day," on May 1, is now an American "institution" as surely as "Wash Day," instituted by the Pilgrim women at Cape Cod, comes on Monday.

It was not Robinson's house, nor the Pesyn Hof, standing on the old site, which the American envoy John Adams, in 1781, visited with emotion, mistakenly supposing that he had entered the Pilgrims' place of meeting. The building in which John and Abigail Adams stood was that wherein the English and Scottish Presbyterians worshiped,—the old Veiled Nuns' Cloister. As a matter of fact, the Pilgrim property passed from the hands of the "Brownists" in 1637, after Jepson, the last owner, had died. While William Penn was in Holland, gathering his Dutch emigrants to help in founding Pennsylvania, Robinson's house and some others were, in whole or in part, taken down. In the Hof, on the site of the little Pilgrim settlement, was erected a Home for Aged Persons of Walloon Extraction. As such it stands to-day, doing, with the forty or more similar settlements in Leyden, its noble work of charity. No country takes better care of its poor than Nederland. On the outer walls of this house, and of St. Peter's Church opposite, are American tablets in honor of Robinson.

In true primitive and apostolical fashion, this church in Robinson's house dwelt in the unity of the Spirit and in the bonds of peace. Members of the Reformed churches of England, Scotland, France, and the Netherlands were received into communion. The Pilgrim congregation, though at its core English, was as cosmopolitan as Christianity itself, having in its membership the representatives of seven nations, four from the islands and at least three from the continent. Its bond of union was not in a set of logical propositions, or a creed in a form of words, but in a covenant of mutual love and service, and of loyalty to the Divine Master. Under the training of their noble, self-effacing pastor, who ever charged them to receive the truth by whatever channel it should come to them, they throve in all holy virtues and graces. Robinson "was very confident that the Lord had more truth and light to break forth out of his holy Word."

CHAPTER XI

LIFE UNDER A FEDERAL GOVERNMENT

ONE darling hope and set purpose of these Leyden upholders of the primitive democracy of the church of Christ was that they might propagate their doctrines. Dwelling in a community where printers and cheap printing materials abounded, they had an inviting opportunity to fulfill their mission by means of the types. There was no absolute liberty anywhere in Europe during the early seventeenth century, but perhaps the largest measure of it was in the Dutch republic, and of this liberty the Pilgrims took advantage. The Dutch being as Gentiles, these gospellers would preach first to those of their own household in the English home-land.

It is not surprising, therefore, that so early as October, 1616, Elder Brewster, who had heretofore supported himself comfortably by teaching the English language to Danes and Germans, began printing books containing those sentiments which were in advance of his time, but which are now widely accepted. Thomas Brewer furnished the money, and William Brewster set up the type. This work infuriated King James of England, who set his envoy at the Hague, Sir Dudley Carleton, on a chase after Brewster, which led to a lively game of hide and seek.

The facts make an interesting narrative, which may be read almost in full in Professor Arber's book, "The Story of the Pilgrim Fathers," but the limits of this work do not allow the space for its recital. At least fifteen books, "if not more, were produced in the thirty-three months, at the furthest, between October, 1616, and June, 1619, both inclusive." Most of these were "Brownist" books, which contained sentiments that are perfectly harmless in a free country, but which were regarded then as moral dynamite.

One or two of the pamphlets (by the Rev. David Calderwood) which Brewster printed exposed King James's political chicanery in attempting, at the Perth Assembly, to compel the Scottish churches to conform to the Anglican establishment. These Leyden "libels" nearly drove James Stuart crazy. His ambassador, Sir Dudley Carleton, had all Amsterdam, Leyden, and Middelburg ransacked to find the printer. Brewster, having gone to England to attend to the scheme of emigrating to America, escaped the fury, but Brewer was seized in his stead, and the types were confiscated. From July, 1619, to February, 1620, there was a lively tilt in politics and diplomacy between the monarchy and the republic, which powerfully excited the Pilgrims and illustrated to them both the charms and the perils of federal government. For Brewer the result was a journey to England under the protection of the Dutch republic, at his sovereign's expense; but the ability of Carleton and great friendship of Maurice, the stadholder, finally enabled James to gain his main point — the restriction of libels against the sovereign of England, then the chief ally of the Dutch republic.

If any one thing convinced the wavering members and decided the Pilgrim company to emigrate as a body, it must have been this seizing of their elder's types and the malignant determination of their "dread sovereign" to destroy even themselves if possible. The stoppage of their printing press meant the end of all propagation of their principles and the carrying out of the missionary idea, which with the Pilgrims were supreme. They had no thought of converting the Dutch people. It was England and their own countrymen whom they had hoped to enlighten and influence. Now this hope was blasted. The Pilgrim press was at an end. A ship must wait upon them, that they might do their work beyond the Atlantic.

The year 1619 was one of continual excitement to the Pilgrim company. Besides the royal chase after Brewster, the affair of Brewer, and the destruction of their printing operations, there was a tremendous commotion in church and state.

The real question at issue in 1619 in the Dutch republic was much the same as that settled in 1865 in the American republic, the preservation of the Union. The decision in both cases was that the central government had a right to be superior to the various states which composed the Union, and to compel their obedience. In the one case slavery was the pretext, in the other theology.

Leyden was the focus of the excitement. In this city the two places and edifices where theology and State-right had their citadels were the university on the one hand, and the City Hall on the other. It was just between the two, not much over a quarter of a mile from either, and in the thoroughfare between them, that the Pilgrims lived.

From first to last the Pilgrims were no doubt unanimously on the side of the Unionists in politics and of the Calvinists in theology. They were opposed, both socially and politically, to the Arminians.

In 1579 the Dutch provinces, or states, had formed at Utrecht a federation, with a written constitution in twenty-six articles. The act and document were referred to as "The Union of Utrecht," and the city was called "The Old Cradle of Liberty." At first the government of the Dutch United States issued its commissions in the name of Philip of Spain, just as the English Parliament, during the English Civil War, issued theirs in the name of Charles I., and the authorities of Massachusetts and the Continental Congress in 1775 wrote theirs in the name of George III. Even Leyden University was, according to a fiction of law, founded in the name of Philip of Spain. This ruler, who was not king of the country, but only Count of Holland, though spoken of in the charter as a benignant protector, would gladly have burned up the Protestant university with all the professors and students inside of it.

In 1581 the Dutch United States dropped the legal fiction and declared themselves forever free of Spain. With this declaration of independence, as well as with the national Dutch flag, the red, white, and blue, the Pilgrims were sufficiently familiar. In the Union of Utrecht, or the written constitution, it had been agreed by Article XIII. that each province should have a right to regulate its own religious affairs, but at that time the only religions then in mind were Romanism and Calvinism. The Arminians claimed that this thirteenth article referred to any religion, or at least any phase of the Christian religion in its Protestant form. The Calvinists insisted that it meant only the Reformed religion, which they identified with Calvinism. Just here was the point at issue, the hinge on which the question of national or of state sovereignty and of orthodoxy or heterodoxy should turn. Roughly speaking, on one side were the people and nation at large, the Calvinists ; on the other were the aristocratic elements, Arminians and stanch upholders of State-right, among whom were many unselfish patriots and earnest Christians.

To understand the situation, we must go back to the century before and see how the Netherlanders changed their views, or rather grew out of the Roman Catholic form of Christianity into that which is founded upon the Scriptures alone.

It has been demonstrated by the late Dr. de Hoop Scheffer that the Reformation among the masses of the Dutch people was, first of all, wrought by the people called Anabaptists. Under William the Silent in the year 1577, they were protected in that noble order of his to the magistrates at Middelburg, which is one of the landmarks in modern history and one of the spiritual corner-stones of the Dutch and American republics : —

"We declare to you that you have no right to interfere with the conscience of any one, so long as he has done nothing that works injury to another person, or a public scandal."

This was eight years before William Brewster, with Secretary Davison, made his first visit into the Netherlands, as we have seen, and thirty-three years before Roger Williams, the apostle of "soul-liberty," was born. To this day, as for over three centuries and a half, the Mennonites, the successors of the "Anabaptists," are numerous and influential in the Netherlands.

The next reformatory wave in the Netherlands was the Lutheran, which influenced many people of the better classes, the wealthy merchants, but did not become in any sense national or general.

The third tidal wave, which is the most potent of the three movements, was that propagated by Calvin, and the men of like mind from the city republic of Geneva. This system of doctrines harmonized most subtly with the Dutch temperament and character. If any one to-day, confused, as so many Americans and English are, as to the difference between Dutchmen and Germans, would make the demarcation clear, let him note but one fact. Roughly speaking, the Germans are Lutherans, the Dutch are Calvinists. Calvinism is almost invariably democratic in spirit and republican in form.

It was by no accident that the ultra-democratic doctrines, both of the "Anabaptists" and of Calvinism, came from the Swiss republic, or federation of states, and were so eagerly embraced by the Dutch. In all federal governments there must be toleration of various ideas and opinions, and both Switzerland and the Dutch republic well illustrate this truth. The fact that a few of the Highland Scots, who in the days of the clan system and semi-feudalism rallied around the

Stuart pretender, "Bonnie Prince Charlie," were Calvinists, forms no true exception to the rule that Calvinism is the nurse of democracy and freedom.

The Arminians took their name from James Arminius, professor of theology in Leyden. He was a noble and aspiring servant of God who loved his fellow men. When a boy, living at Oudewater, the Spaniards had captured the town and massacred the people, and he was left an orphan. He grew up a bright student and became a noble citizen and patriot. He secured the repeal of hostile legislation against the Jews, and was always warmly in favor of full toleration. When made professor he began to modify the strict system of Calvin. His rival and opponent, Professor Gomarus, opened a public controversy with him. The discussions soon passed out beyond the scholastic and aristocratic circles and down among the common people. The whole nation became a school of thought and argument on one of the greatest themes that can occupy the mind of man — the reconciliation of human free will with the divine sovereignty. Arminius did not live to see his doctrines and those of Calvin forged into political weapons and his countrymen on the brink of civil war. He died October 19, 1609, while the Pilgrims were in Amsterdam. It was nearly a century and a half afterwards that John Wesley in England preached a form of Christianity quite other than that of the Dutch divine, which is called "Arminianism."

By the year 1615 the lines of division in the Dutch republic showed that on one side were ranged the rich and wealthy people of the cities and those influential in municipal councils and state governments, especially in the mighty single State of Holland. These were the Arminians and men emphasizing State-right. These suspected that the ambition of the stadholder was to become a king and to destroy the republic and local freedom. They feared that the soldier would override law, and the sword dictate both might and right.

On the other hand were the masses of the people at large, led and directed at first by their domines, or pastors, and afterwards by the stadholder and his advisers. At first the question was purely theological; but where State and Church are united, and the life of one seems to depend upon the life of the other, it is not possible to keep theology and politics apart. It is, as state churchmen fear, very much as in the case of the Siamese twins, — the death of one is the death of the other, though the experience of the American republic proves that this is not necessarily so. At first, also, as there seems little reason to doubt, the Arminians, having wealth and power on their side, were oppressive and overbearing. The Calvinists were almost fanatical Union men, and suspected that the Arminians were at heart secessionists and would sell out to Spain. They called Barneveldt a pope, a tyrant, and a traitor. So far as we can judge, he was a sincere patriot, though not a statesman of deep insight, nor of sympathy with the commons. He was a man of precedents, unable to see or measure new forces. He had opposed Leicester and the "English party." In many respects he was a public functionary of consummate ability and unceasing industry. Intellectually he was an agnostic, his motto being "To know nothing is the safest faith."

The two leaders in whom the conflicting principles were incarnated were Maurice, the soldier, and Barneveldt, the statesman. The former was a young man of splendid military abilities, though not of pure private life; the latter was a sage in years and of stainless private character. The one was the head of the Union army and the stadholder of several of the States. The other was the soul of the legislature of Holland and the ablest man in the national congress, or States-General. On the 4th of August, 1617, the issue between union and secession seemed squarely drawn, when, after Maurice's military demonstration in the Cloister church at the Hague, the legislature of Holland, at Barneveldt's motion, passed the famous Sharp Resolve, which stated the doctrine of State sovereignty in its plainest form. Then began the enrollment and training of State militia in the interest of State-right and possibly of secession.

In Leyden and Utrecht the partisans of Barneveldt were most numerous, and here the waartgelders, or State militia, were in greatest force. In front of and surrounding the City Hall in Leyden had been built a strong fort of oak beams bolted together and furnished with iron prongs to prevent escalade. This fort was mounted with cannon and garrisoned by Arminian militia. During the troubles several citizens were killed. With bloodshed so very near their own doors, and the flames of civil war apparently ready to burst out, what wonder is it that at this very time the Pilgrims began action which ended in their settlement in America? Between King James and Dutch deviltry there seemed little to choose but the deep sea.

There must have been lively talk at the Pilgrim supper tables when day's work was over, on the evening of October 23, 1618. Fences, curbstones, and walls were plastered with political squibs, rhymes, and caricatures of the opposing parties, but on the whole they pointed to the waning fortunes of the Arminians. On the previous evening, Maurice, the Union general, had sent some companies of national troops to garrison the city. The supremacy of the red, white, and blue flag, the Union banner, over the lion flag of the State of Holland, was demonstrated in Leyden, as it was soon to be over that of the cross and shield of Utrecht.

On the next day the Arminian cause in Leyden was dead beyond power of resurrection. Maurice came to the City Hall with his staff and force, all in their brilliant uniforms and amid an immense crowd of people. The city magistracy was changed. The palisade, or fort, which had been dubbed "Barneveldt's teeth," was torn to pieces by the people, who dragged the timber and iron to the market-place, where they were sold at auction for fuel or souvenirs. It was a day of great popular rejoicing in Leyden, and in the general delight there is little doubt that some of the Pilgrim men and boys had their share.

The people in the seven States of the republic had refused to take the decision of a provincial synod, or to have a single State like Holland settle the questions at issue. They demanded the voice of the whole nation in council and the ultimatum of the national church. The great national Synod of Dordrecht, "the only Protestant Œcumenical Council," was therefore called. It was opened on Monday, November 13, 1618, with delegates from nearly all the countries and states in which there were Reformed churches, including Great Britain, which sent over several eminent men. These sat at a table by themselves and received extra pay, allowances, and gifts, the party in power being very anxious to keep the friendship of King James.

The synod was in its management wholly a political affair and the creation of the Dutch Congress. It had but one purpose — the condemnation of the Arminians and the strengthening of the national power. After one hundred and nineteen sessions held in the Artillery Armory at Dordrecht, the synod concluded with its famous declarations called the Canons of the Synod of Dort. The Arminian ministers had their salaries paid, and being invited to leave the country, they did so. They were in all about two hundred in number, and most of them went out quietly and peaceably. They were not harassed or persecuted, as were the Dissenters at this time in England; they were only shut off from the state church patronage.

Maurice was very slow in forming a judgment or entering upon a line of policy; but when once his mind was made up, he was in action as quick as lightning and implacable as death. Confronted by threats of secession and seeing, as he believed, the raising of troops to resist the Union, he drew the sword.

Barneveldt, on the charge of a purpose to "plunge the nation into a blood bath," had been arrested and imprisoned, August 29, 1618. The question was now what to do with him. As the synod progressed, and Maurice felt his course approved, so also the tribunal created to try Barneveldt became more ready to yield to popular clamor. The judges found him guilty, and Maurice ordered his execution. On the 13th of May, 1619, four days after the adjournment of the Synod of Dort, the aged statesman was beheaded in the public square of the Binnenhof at the Hague. This unnecessary act was probably a judicial murder. It was accomplished in the presence of thousands of spectators, including a body of English troops, among whose officers may have been Miles Standish.

To those who can understand the situation, there is little difficulty in seeing why John Robinson was strenuously a Calvinist and in favor both of the Synod of Dort and of its doctrines, and why the members of the Pilgrim company, very probably in overwhelming majority if not to a man, approved of the action of Maurice, and took the Union side. No one need make any apology for the Pilgrims in this, unless he is determined to judge the seventeenth by the light of the nineteenth century.

It is very probable that Robinson attended some of the sessions of the synod. He certainly entered heart and soul into the controversy. Bradford says that he "was an acute and expert disputant, very quick and ready, and had much bickering with the Arminians, who stood more in fear of him than of any of the university of Leyden."

Governor Winslow also says, "And our Pastor, Master Robinson, in the time when Arminianism prevailed so much, at the request of the most orthodox divines as Polyander, Festus Hommius, etc., disputed daily in the academy at Leyden against Episcopius and others, the grand champions of that error, and had as good respect amongst them as any of their own divines." Indeed, Robinson had attended the lectures on both sides of the controversy, in order to make up his mind.

It is idle to identify or even make close comparison of the Dutch political Arminianism of the period from A. D. 1609 to 1621, with the theological system of Wesley and the Methodist Christians.

Whatever may be the relative merits of the theological controversy, into which we cannot here enter, it is hard to see how the Leyden company, being lovers of freedom and the pure gospel, could be anything else than what they were. They saw, or thought they saw, that the tendency of Arminianism then was *not*, as perhaps Barneveldt saw or thought, to the prevalence of the civil spirit over militarism, and law over war, to toleration and freedom, to the sure maintenance of local rights in politics and of the conscience in religion, to national wealth, peace, and unity, but wholly to the contrary.

The Pilgrim company, with the Dutch Calvinists, believed that Calvinism and union meant right thinking and right living before God, a strengthened and purified nation, supremacy of the national over the local and state government, freedom from Rome, the humiliation of Spain, colonization of America, and a free development of the human spirit in all departments of activity, especially in schools, education, and everything that uplifts the plain people. To them the triumph of the Union meant democracy and the rights of the people, as well as orthodoxy in religion. It is very probable that these exiles for conscience' sake rejoiced equally with the natives at the issue. Probably no man understood the whole situation better than Elder Brewster, John Robinson, and William Bradford. Their feeling toward Maurice was probably much like that which John Bright in our day had for Abraham Lincoln or Ulysses Grant.

CHAPTER XII

THE DEBATE UPON EMIGRATION

ONE notable point at issue between Barneveldt and Maurice was over a matter that directly concerned the Pilgrim company and influenced their future. The Dutch Calvinists believed, with Maurice, in colonization. Barneveldt and his partisans did not. Long before the West India Company was actually chartered under that name, the Hollanders began the agitation about settling New Netherland. During the time of truce, between 1609 and 1621, it would have been an act of war for the Dutch to send emigrants to the Hudson River region, because Spain claimed all North America. But though they would not break faith by taking action, they discussed the matter. Among the first, so early as 1615, to plan a colony beyond sea, was Jesse de Forest, one of the several hundred Walloons living in Leyden, working side by side with the English dyers and silk-workers, his place of worship being but a few feet away from Robinson's home.

As Maurice, Prince of Orange, is in a large sense the founder of New York State, so is Jesse de Forest of New York City. De Forest was born at Avesnes, in Hainault, from which province many Protestant refugees reached England. Many Americans, as well as English folk, descended from these now spell their names Haines, Hanway, Hanna, or with some other variation. Of good social connections, the parents of Jesse de Forest left their native city, probably to escape religious prosecution, and arrived at Leyden in 1603, living there a year and a half, and then going to Amsterdam. Gerard de Forest, brother of Jesse, lived in Leyden from 1605 to 1654, as a dyer. Jesse is found in Leyden in February, 1615, where one of his children was baptized. A few months later, in July, he applied to Sir Dudley Carleton, asking assistance by which his company might get to Virginia, there being fifty-six Walloon families wanting to go. But King James, though he was willing to grant permission, refused assistance, and the project failed. It was not until 1622 that de Forest was able to carry out his scheme. The ship New Netherland in March, 1623, carried to Manhattan Island and the Walloon's Boght, or bend, now called Wallabout in Brooklyn, thirty families, and thus began the settlement of New Netherland and the great Empire State.

How early the Pilgrims began to talk of finding a new home, and one as far as possible out of the direct reach of King James and the persecuting bishops, is not known. Between the Spaniards and King James there was little to choose, but where should they go? Ireland and Zealand were proposed, and so was Venezuela. Zealand seemed rather a congenial home, for the Sabbath laws were very strict there, but land was high, and English people would sooner or later become Dutch.

There had been many attempts to plant an English colony upon the American shores, but none had proved a success until that started at Jamestown. Even this had many troubles and trials, and its continued existence was still very uncertain at the time when the Pilgrims were becoming restless with schemes of migration. With the Spanish war against the Dutch about to open, and King James and his bishops rampant and making their lives dangerous; between the difficulty of some of their less qualified members in getting a living, — they having been not skilled mechanics, but only plain country people, — and the probability of losing their names and their language, and being submerged among the Dutch people, like "the ten lost tribes of Israel;" the small likelihood of enforcing their notions of Sabbath-keeping upon the Dutch; the inability of their leading men, Robinson, Brewster, Winslow, Bradford and others, to give such an English education to their children as they themselves had received or now desired; and last but not least, with their press or social means of propagating their ideas destroyed—it is no wonder they longed to make a change. They yearned to go where they could keep alive their convictions and propagate their ideas of church government and practical Christianity; but to go to Jamestown, where the political bishops could touch them, would be hardly better than returning to England.

Through Sir Edwin Sandys, their friend, or at least the friend of Brewster, they learned that the sovereign would grant no freedom of conscience in America. After thinking it over, King James referred their request for toleration to the Archbishop of Canterbury and the Bishop of London. This was like recommending lambs to wolves. They soon found that no Brownists or Separatists need apply to go to the James River country. There was already a Virginia Company formed, but it was divided into two hostile factions. One party represented the nobler and progressive, and the other reactionary and unlovely England, and the former befriended the Leyden Separatists. Hard as it was for the Pilgrims to resolve to try the ocean and wilderness, they found it, as Bradford says, harder than they expected to get leave and opportunity to go.

Robinson was probably one of the first to decide upon removal elsewhere. He is known to have spoken of his design of founding a free religious colony to two of his Dutch friends, Professor A. Walaens and Daniel Festus Hommius. When the directors of the New Netherland Trading Company heard through these two gentlemen of Robinson's desire, they made "large offers," as Bradford says, promising not only to give the Pilgrim colonists free passage to America, but also to furnish every family with cattle. Robinson thought at that time that about four hundred families from Holland and England would form the settlement. Since these Pilgrims had an excellent reputation in Leyden for honesty, diligence, and general good character, and most of them knew Dutch pretty well, they would make first-rate colonists. The directors of the New Netherland company, on February 20, 1620, applied to Maurice, the stadholder, telling about this English preacher of Leyden who was versed in the Dutch language. They asked permission not only to plant the colony, but also requested that two Dutch men-of-war might convey the colonists to New Netherland. With Spanish cruisers on the seas and King James ready to seize these people as his prey, danger must be provided against.

When looked at by Maurice and the States-General in a political and diplomatic light, the proposition to transport these Englishmen to America was something quite the reverse of what had been seen through the rosy commercial medium of the Amsterdam directors. In the first place, it was not certain but that King James, on the strength of the fact that Henry Hudson was an Englishman, might claim New Netherland as English property. Ridiculous though the idea might seem to be, the English government had detained the Half Moon upon its arrival at Plymouth en route for Amsterdam; and although the ship and crew reached home, it is not certain that Henry Hudson ever got again to Holland. Furthermore, the idea of offending both Spain and King James at once could not be entertained. The "Spanish party" was at this time very powerful at the English court, and King James was angling for the alliance of one of his children with a Spanish princess. To help openly and directly a nest of heretics who had printed books which stung King James and angered him beyond the telling, so that he wanted to seize the authors and printers and have "the Devil rive their souls and bodies all in collops and cast them into hell," would be a suicidal policy. It would have looked exactly like a personal insult to the British James, the seeking of a quarrel, and a direct defiance of the government at London, thus to have any official sanction given at the Hague to this company of Englishmen. A scheme which would not only give the Separatists aid and comfort, but which required the employment of war-ships of the republic to cover and protect them under its flag, could not be tolerated for a moment.

Then the war with Spain was to be resumed in a few months, and every man and ship, cartridge and cannon, was urgently needed at home. The petition of the directors of the New Netherland company was therefore denied. Robinson, who knew local and foreign politics so well, must have foreseen the issue; for prior to the stadholder's decision, negotiations had been opened, most probably through Brewster, with the Virginia Company in London.

Brewster in England had one strong and generous friend in Sir Edwin Sandys, whom we may call one of the political forefathers of the United States of America. When president of the Virginia Company in 1620, he introduced the Frisian custom of unconstrained and secret voting by means of the written ballot. He was a son of the Archbishop of York, Edwin Sandys, who in 1576 had appointed Brewster's father as his agent at Scrooby. Before his death, the archbishop had transferred the manor to his son, Sir Samuel Sandys, who was Brewster's landlord. Sir Edwin Sandys, the brother of Samuel, a liberal member of the government, opposed the "Spanish party" at court, secured the foundation of a constitutional state with a representative government in Virginia, and laid generous plans for the Pilgrims' proposed settlement in America. It was he who obtained two patents for the Plymouth Colony. It was probably Sir Edwin Sandys, as Dr. Edward Eggleston suggests, who lent the Leyden congregation three hundred pounds without interest for three years, and this sum, when the Pilgrims could get no rates better than those of Asiatic money-lenders, was equal to about five thousand dollars in our money of to-day. In all probability it was Sir Edwin Sandys's aid in friendship and money that enabled and decided the Pilgrim company to embark for America.

After prayer, conference, and a sermon from Robinson, on the text in 1 Samuel xxiii. 3. 4, the younger and stronger portion of the company decided that their Judah was Leyden and their Keilah was in America, and that between King James and the Spaniards there was little difference. So trusting in God they resolved to sail.

Mr. Thomas Weston, a London merchant, and about seventy other Englishmen planned an emigration scheme at ten pounds a share. Each colonist was to be allowed to work two days in a week for his own benefit. At the end of seven years, the profits on the total possessions and earnings of the colonists were to be divided between the colony and the corporation. On this basis articles were signed.

While Carver and Cushman went over to England to get the money and to charter a ship and equip it with provisions, those who were bent on going, — the strongest, bravest, and most of them the younger ones, — began to prepare, selling off everything except what they might need for the voyage and for life in the New World. Weston's company was called the Merchant Adventurers, and their great idea was to get money through the fisheries and farming in New England and by means of the work of the Pilgrims or other colonists. The Adventurers got fresh powers from the Plymouth company and a patent granting a measure of self-government, and also, with what must have seemed tremendous English impudence and unscrupulousness to the Dutchmen, the right to land near the mouth of the Hudson River.

In order to get reënforcements of colonists from England, Carver and Cushman associated Christopher Martin to carry out their arrangements. If we are to believe Cushman, this Mr. Martin, of Essex, proved to be a bad-tempered and impracticable man. When the Merchant Adventurers met with Cushman, they wanted an alteration in the original terms which showed great greediness in these speculators; and Cushman, without consulting the Leyden people or his joint representatives, agreed to it. By this, each colonist was obliged to work every day in the week except Sundays, having no time to himself. The whole of the work and profits of the colonists, going into a common fund, was to be equally divided at the end of seven years between the capitalists and the workmen.

As soon as the Leyden company heard of this new contract, they declared that Cushman had made conditions more fit for thieves and slaves than for honest men. Nevertheless they consented to them. Captain John Smith offered his services to the Leyden Pilgrims; but these were declined, possibly because Smith's true character was known to them, but more probably because they had already agreed with Miles Standish that he should be their military commander; and better always one good general than two in command.

In Holland the Speedwell, a pinnace of sixty tons burden, was bought and fitted out, and the English pilot arrived toward the end of May. Among the Leyden men, there were few, if any, — possibly there was not one man, — familiar with ships or sea life. No harpoons or whaling implements and very little fishing tackle seem to have been provided. In their eagerness to get away promptly and across the sea in summer weather, that they might reach the Hudson River region before frost, they made the mistake of ordering for the Speedwell heavier and taller masts and larger spars than her hull had been built to receive, thus altering most unwisely and disastrously her "trim." Bradford says she was "overmasted," but whether in England or Holland is not certain. Captain George Waymouth and Sir Walter Raleigh have left us severe criticisms on the English-built ships of their time, as being of bad proportions, and not being able to bear sail or steer readily, "for want of art in proportioning of the mould and fittings of the mast and tackling." We do not hear of these inveterate landsmen and townsfolk, who were about to venture on the Atlantic, taking counsel of Dutch shipbuilders or mariners as to the proportions of their craft.

When later, however, the English captain, who did not relish going on the voyage, found this out, as he quickly would, he crowded on too much sail so that the hull became as "leaky as a sieve." The Pilgrim experiences with seafaring men do not raise our opinion of the latter. It is a monotonous and discouraging story of dishonesty and profanity. Bradford tells us that the Speedwell was afterwards "sold and put into her old trim;" that is, masts of the right size and weight for the hull were set in. Then "she made many voyages, and performed her service very sufficiently; to the great profit of her owners." It is even possible that from this mistake of the Leyden landsmen, the subsequent miseries and troubles of the seafaring passengers and sick, starving, and dying colonists came. Professor Arber, who calls the captain a "rascal," says: "For this fatuous and supreme error of judgment in business matters, and all that came of it, the Leyden church alone was responsible. No one in England had anything to do with it." All of which, so long as we do not know every detail, *may* be true.

Both Speedwell and Mayflower are names of well-known plants and blossoms in England, though the name "Mayflower" is wholly a popular, rather than a scientific or botanical term. In England it may be the hawthorn, the cuckoo flower, the marsh marigold, or it may be something else; in the United States it is the trailing arbutus. The name Mayflower was exceedingly common among English ships. Two of Drake's vessels were so named, and there were many others called the Mayflower in the records of the British navy and merchant marine.

The speedwell is an herb, with creeping and ascending stem, and bright blue flowers in the raceme or on a stalk. In England it is also named the eye-bright, to say nothing of the terms angel's eye, God's eye, bird's eye, and so on, each of which was called the speedwell. There were various varieties of the flower and of the one which was formerly much used in medicine. Neither Bradford nor Mourt refers to the names of these historic ships; but we find the more famous one mentioned in the Plymouth records: "The falls (apportionments) of their grounds, which came first over in the Mayflower: according as their lots were cast, 1623." The Speedwell is first named in Nathaniel Morton's book "The New England's Memorial."

When all was ready, it was resolved that those who should go on the Speedwell, before others should follow, should be the youngest and strongest; second, they must be volunteers; and if a majority went, Robinson should go with them; and if a minority, Elder Brewster. If the voyage turned out disastrously, — "if the Lord should frown upon our proceedings," — then those remaining in Leyden should help those that returned; but "if God should be pleased to favor them that went, then they also should endeavor to help over such as was poor and ancient and willing to come." When it came to vote, the majority agreed to stay for a while, all except a very few intending ultimately to cross the Atlantic.

So it came to pass that the pinnace at Delfshaven was the pioneer of a Pilgrim fleet, consisting of the Speedwell, Mayflower, Fortune, Anne, Little James, Mayflower 2d (1629), and the Handmaid (1630). The affectionate term "Pilgrim Fathers," coined by later generations, includes (1) the members of the Leyden church who voted for emigration, whether able or unable to go; (2) those who came from England and joined the church. The Mayflower passengers constituted the "Old Stock" of Bradford's naming. Those who reached New Plymouth in the Mayflower, Anne, and Little James were called the "Old Comers," or "Forefathers."

CHAPTER XIII

WESTWARD HO!

THE inland voyage of the Pilgrims, from the Nun's Bridge on the Rapenburg in Leyden to Delfshaven, was twenty-four miles in length. The route is parallel with the lines of the modern rail and tram roads, and in the form of an obtuse angle, or like a widened-out *V*, the point being a little below the Hague. The waters to be traversed were the Vliet and the Schie. They first moved southwestwardly eleven miles, skirting a morass, now the dry and green Veen or Fen polder, until near Ryswick, and then southwestwardly directly through the city of Delft. At the village of Overschie, they went straight forward to Delfshaven, on arriving at which, they had voyaged alongside of or through three "lands," — Rhineland, Westland, and Schieland.

The haven of Delft, or Delfshaven (Delft's Haven), was a pretty little town founded in the fourteenth century, where were early erected the chapel of St. Anthony and other buildings which, when the men with their faces set towards America arrived there, had already seen the sunsets of three hundred years. It had its own burgomaster, council, and "arms" — a three-banded shield showing, between herring and wheat, a centre of alternate strips of white and green. The motto on the seal of the brick church, past which the Pilgrims sailed, reads "The haven of salvation alone with God of Zion is."

Coming from Leyden it could not be otherwise than that these people, at least half of whom, perhaps, had been born in Holland and talked Dutch, would know the story of the land and water over which they sailed. A generation or two before, and during the siege of Leyden, the great dike through which, by lock and sluice, they were now to pass had been cut to let in the water to "over-stream" the whole country up to the beleaguered city, in order to bring in the relief ships. Between Overschie and Delfshaven the makers of New Plymouth floated high above the pastures below them, for here the dikes rise in a great mass above what is one of the lowest portions of the Low Countries, much of the land being sixteen feet beneath the unit of level or high-tide mark at Amsterdam. The great sea dike, which runs from the seacoast forty miles into the country, has intrusted to it the safety of the whole country of South Holland from the Maas River to Leyden.

The Pilgrim pioneers had a night to pass in Delfshaven. Where and how did they spend it? Fortunately, as Bradford says, they found the ship and all things ready. There was probably little sleep for the most of them, who made the hours speed along "with friendly entertainment and Christian discourse and other real expressions of true Christian love." There is no record for or against the pretty but baseless tradition that the Speedwell passengers and their friends held a farewell meeting in the Reformed church of Delfshaven. The Book of the Minutes of the Consistory covering the year 1620 is not known to be in existence, having disappeared some years later (1634–1642) during the disputes, or "twisten," between the authorities of the church and the city. Intrinsic probability is against the idea. The local tradition is possibly a true one, that most of the emigrants and their friends slept in one of the warehouses of the Netherlands Trading Company. These were on the banks of the canal near the ship's anchorage. Possibly some of the passengers or their friends occupied the boats and storage houses or huts closer to the landing.

To-day the chief sights for the tourist in Delfshaven are, besides the church, the birthplace and the statue of Piet Heyn, the admiral who in 1628 captured the Spanish silver fleet. The maps of Delfshaven in 1620, in the Water-State office, show that the frontage of the city and the lines of the quays and wharves were quite different from what they are to-day. The imposing windmills now built near the river were not then in existence. Nevertheless, the chief canal, streets, and older quays were much the same as at present. Out in the river there was then free course of deep flowing water, where to-day there is a long island. This accumulation of silt could, by the year 1761, be sailed over only at high water. It is now grass-grown and even hilly. It is pierced in the centre with a sluice called the Schiemond, or mouth of the Schie, and the whole western half of the double island called Riuge Platt (Rough Place) is occupied by various dwellings or edifices of industry. The avenue, lined with trees and having a southern exposure, fronts the main channel of the Maas River, and was (in July, 1892) appropriately named by the burgomaster and city council of Rotterdam, of which Delfshaven is now a part, "Pelgrim Kade;" that is, Pilgrim Avenue or Quay.

In picturing to our minds the departure of the Pilgrims, we cannot imagine the elegantly dressed ladies and gentlemen with feathers and silks and jewels such as we see in some highly idealized pictures, any more than we can conjure up, as a certain lithographer once did, two full-rigged ships with a vast crowd of people in boats waving farewells, or the imaginary rocks and high lands which exist on canvas, but not in reality. It is more than probable that the picture painted by the Cuyps, father and son, gives the exact facts.

This painting, small in size, superb in color, and lively in detail, represents, with the usual Dutch realism, a gay horse and horseman, the inevitable little dog, a Diana-like huntress, with boy carrying her birds, arms, and case, in the foreground, and a group of sheds or huts, serving as storehouses for cargoes and naval goods, at the end of a quay. It gives no hint of any island such as now fronts Delfshaven, and which one sees as he enters or leaves Rotterdam on the steamers of the Dutch or Holland-America line. The buildings were not splendid affairs of masonry, brick, and iron, as to-day. The woodcuts and paintings of the period depict them as they were. In garb of dark or brown clothes of the rigid style and cut of English Puritans, with high and wide-rimmed black hats, with ruffs around their necks, a company of men numbering a dozen or so, with a boy or two, are walking down toward the end of the pier. A big Dutch porter-woman in front and a porter-man at the rear carry big bundles for them. Three or four of the party have muskets, and one, a short, doughty figure, with his legs covered with long high cordovan leather boots, holds his arms akimbo and wears a sword. In the middle, arm in arm with the mate or captain, both of whom are dressed not as Puritans, but as ship folk, is a man with a round or melon-shaped cap, such as clergymen wore in those days. This is not Elder Brewster, who probably wore no special costume, and who was then, as we think, hiding in England, but the Rev. John Robinson. About the cabins or storehouses on the shore are more emigrants, and among the shipping to the left, beside the tricolor Dutch flags on the vessels sailing, or about to sail, is a heavily masted pinnace, lying on the low but rising tide, apparently of about sixty tons burden. Out of her sides are poked the noses of three cannons. On board are many people, among whom are gayly dressed English sailors. Though the Dutch flag flies conspicuously, yet toward the bow is carved the beast best known in English heraldry. This rampant red lion, the shape and rig of the vessel, its abundance of color, and the gay dress of the crew tell of an English ship of the model of Elizabethan or Jacobean times.

Evidently the situation here is as usual with the Pilgrim company. The women and children and most of the party are already on board, and the leading men, Robinson, Bradford, Standish, and others, are the last to attend to details and to embark. The tide is rising, but much shore space is yet exposed that is to be covered at flood.

Before the main body of the resolute voyagers parted from their friends there were farewells, with sighs, and sobs, and prayers, and tears gushing from every eye, and pithy speeches piercing every heart. Some of the people of Delfshaven who stood by on the quay, moved with sympathy, could not refrain from tears. These English people in the pioneer ship were going out, as they thought, to New Netherland, to the wild country across the Atlantic, and this time little Delfshaven had a scene such as was common at the Weepers' Tower in metropolitan Amsterdam. Long afterwards, when Winslow wrote of the incident, he said that the memory of the first Pilgrims' parting (for the several other ships which reached Plymouth later doubtless sailed from Delfshaven) was still fresh among the people of this port on the Maas.

The tide, which waits for no man, had risen; Robinson and the few friends who had come on board must disembark. So falling on his knees, and they all with him, with watery cheeks, their pastor commended them with most fervent prayers to the Lord for his blessing. These were Englishmen who were not afraid to shed tears. Before the ship passed out of the haven into the river, the armed men in the company "gave them a volley of small shot and [the sailors fired] three pieces of ordnance." Then lifting up their hands one to another, that is, waving farewells, the ship moved out on the bosom of the Maas, sailing over water where now is solid land, then down the river and past the Hook of Holland into the German Ocean. The Pilgrim church was now half on land and half on sea.

To-day, as the passengers on the Dutch steamers of the Netherlands-American Steam Navigation Company enter or leave Rotterdam, they may easily see, while on the Maas River, the exact place whence the Speedwell sailed out, for the sluice piercing the island in the centre enables one to look into and up the very canal and at the street and quays whence the departure took place.

The Speedwell, leaving Delfshaven on Saturday, the 1st of August, *might* have joined the Mayflower at Southampton on the following Wednesday, August 5. Had the two ships been able to sail promptly, the united company could have reached the Hudson River region in time to be well housed before winter. It was not so to be.

After a joyful welcome and mutual congratulations from their English friends, including probably Elder Brewster, the Leyden people fell to parley about their business and how to dispatch it with the best expedition. Then their troubles broke out afresh, for they were vexed about the stipulations, Weston having changed the original agreement. The Speedwell people would not agree with the new conditions without the consent of those left behind in Leyden, and, indeed, they had been charged not to do so. At this Weston was angry, and told them to "stand on their own legs," and went off in a huff: "and whereas there wanted well near one hundred pounds to clear things at their going away; he would not take order to disburse a penny; but let them shift as they could." So the Pilgrims were obliged to sell off three or four score firkins of butter, which fortunately was something of which they had enough and to spare.

A more agreeable incident at Southampton was the engagement of a cooper, who was none other than John Alden. He was a hearty, healthy, and handsome young fellow. As Paul found his Luke at Troas, so Bradford met at Southampton his future companion and helper of unfailing fidelity.

Ale or beer being then part of daily diet, a cooper was indispensable. Furthermore, no vessel carrying kegs or barrels could leave port without giving surety to import into England as much timber for staves, then called "clapboard," as had been used in making the kegs or barrels exported. The Pilgrim ships could not have sailed without a cooper, for the law was explicit. Part of the statute of Parliament passed in 1543 reads: —

"Every Artificer of the Mystery of Coopers may take, for every Beer Barrel by him sold, x. d. and for every Beer Kilderkin, vi. d. Whosoever shall carry Beer beyond Sea, shall find Sureties to the Customers of that Port, to bring in Clapboard meet to make so much Vessel as he shall carry forth."

We shall see that the first load of merchandise

sent home from America by the Pilgrims consisted largely of staves, or "clapboards."

With a governor and two or three assistants for each ship, for good order and the proper use of provisions, which the shipmasters desired and agreed with, they sailed away. The Mayflower was by far the better provisioned, equipped, and armed ship of the two, but, as usual, the noble-hearted leaders went on board the Speedwell. Then, most probably because the rascally captain crowded sail on the overmasted Speedwell, although she had been twice examined and trimmed at much cost at Southampton, she was found, after a day or two, to be unseaworthy. According to Cushman, she was "as open and leaky as a sieve" and in danger of sinking. The captains consulting together, and being near the coast of Devon, they put in at the mouth of the Dart River, though they lost thereby a fair wind, and the poor Pilgrims had to pay the expenses of the stay of ten days at Dartmouth.

Thoroughly searched from stem to stern, the Speedwell's leaks were found and mended. Then they put to sea again on August 23 with good hopes, expecting no more hindrances; but when well out on the Atlantic, Captain Reynolds declared that the Speedwell must bear up or sink at sea. Since no special leak could be found, it was judged that the trouble was on account of the general weakness of the ship. So back they went to Plymouth, where they had to stay some time. While there, they were treated very kindly by the people of the free church, forming what is now the Grange Street Chapel, the Mayflower meanwhile lying off the Barbican.

Plymouth was not then, as it is now, guarded and defended by a massive breakwater of masonry, but only an open roadstead. In time of heavy storms the vessels anchored close together were apt to be knocked to pieces, one against the other, or dashed from the crest of the wave to the ground. Fortunately it was fine weather during the Pilgrims' stay. The Speedwell was sent back to London, and, being remasted, became a seaworthy vessel, as has been said. The Mayflower was to go alone. They stowed on board from the Speedwell whoever and whatever the Mayflower could take. Since none but volunteers were wanted to cross the Atlantic, those discontented or fearful, least useful or most unfit to bear hardships, — some twenty in number, — went back to London.

Thus after delays and disappointments enough to appall the stoutest spirits, the voyage began, all being compact together in one ship. The Mayflower became a floating bethel, and this company of Christians the church on the sea. Sail was set in a prosperous wind. At first they enjoyed fair weather. When starting from Leyden, they had hoped to be in the new world, their third home, before frost; but when in mid-ocean the winds were contrary. The equinoctial storms burst upon them. By this time the Pilgrim leaders, rendered suspicious by their many disappointments at the hands of rascally men, gathered from the mutterings of the sailors that the ship was unseaworthy. In the gale she was strained so badly that one of the main beams amidships was bowed and cracked, so that it looked as if the Mayflower would go to pieces in mid-ocean, or at least that they would have to turn back once more. They even entered into serious consultation with the captain and mates whether they should not, after all, retrace their course, rather than cast themselves into a desperate and inevitable peril. With the shipmen, it was a question between money and life, to lose their contract and wages, or to hazard their lives too desperately.

After considering all phases of the question, the ship's officers, trusting their ship and knowing her to be firm under the water, believed that with proper repairs, and without too heavy a press of sail, they would make the voyage in safety.

Fortunately one of the passengers had brought out of Holland, where, at Delft especially, the natives were famous for ship hardware, a great iron screw. This was probably a "lifting jack," or "jackscrew," called in Dutch a *domme kracht*, or *vijzel*. As cannon were invented before guns or pistols, so the vijzel was a forerunner of the monkey-wrench. The same people who invented the ship's camel invented this, the ship's crutch. Though not usually found on English vessels at that time, lifting jacks were common on Dutch ships, and were used for the very purpose to which this "great screw" of the passenger from Leyden was now put; that is, to force the dislocated beam up and back into place.

This bit of iron turned the scale of decision, and saved to the world—New England. Both the carpenter and the captain agreed that when raised into its place, and a post put under it and set firm into the lower deck, and otherwise bound and buckled together, the timber would be sufficiently secure to remove all cause for anxiety. This work was done, and thereafter they had no further trouble. Furthermore, by calking the decks and upper works there would be no great danger from the waves, though by the straining of the ship in the storm the water still came down into the cabins and below deck, keeping the wretched passengers wet and cold.

In sundry of these storms the seas were so high that they could not bear a knot of sail, but for days together were forced "to hull;" that is, they drifted at the mercy of the wind, or went "scudding under bare poles," while the company was fastened below decks, shivering, seasick, forlorn. In the foul air were bred the germs of that quick consumption of which so many, when on land, were soon to die.

It was during one of these storms that a lively young fellow named John Howland, coming from below the hatches out on deck, was, in the roll of the ship, thrown into the sea. Providentially, at the same time the topsail halyard happened to have broken loose from its belaying pin and was trailing in the sea, and John caught hold of it. In Bradford's words, "He was sundry fathoms under water." He held on till "he was hauled up by the same rope to the brim of the water," and then with a boat-hook was got into the ship again and his life saved. Young Howland was somewhat the worse for his adventure, but lived to be a signer of the immortal compact at Cape Cod, useful in church and commonwealth, and the ancestor of many families.

A sailor, proud of his strength and health, made himself very disagreeable by swearing at the poor seasick passengers, saying he hoped to cast one half of them into the sea. Before the voyage was half over, this hearty wretch was struck with disease, and "he was himself the first that was thrown overboard." We wonder from the description Bradford gives whether he was a hard drinker and died of delirium tremens.

William Button, who was probably a medical student and assistant of the doctor, Samuel Fuller, died on November 16, and his body was committed to the deep. Bradford says nothing about any religious exercises, such as are often so impressive on seaboard on committal of a body to the deep. The Puritans cared next to nothing about ceremonies over a corpse whether at wave or grave. In their reaction against priestcraft they were on principle opposed to all mortuary ritual. Theirs was a religion of life, not of death.

The loss of Dr. Fuller's assistant was made up by the birth at sea of a baby, born of Stephen Hopkins and his wife Elizabeth, and named Oceanus. There were one hundred and two people in the Pilgrim company when they left Plymouth the second time. Early in December Peregrine White was born, making the total number of individuals on the register of the Mayflower company, between old and new Plymouth, one hundred and four, seventy-five males and twenty-nine females. Among the adults were twenty-four heads of households, eighteen wives, thirteen sons or male relatives, seven daughters or other female relatives, fourteen male servants, one female servant, and fifteen single men, making ninety-two in all. There were also nine boys and three girls. Of the ship's officers, Jones was the captain and Coppin a pilot.

CHAPTER XIV

THE COMPACT AT CAPE COD

If the Mayflower had started out with a pilot who had been inside Sandy Hook, her passengers would probably have had no difficulty in reaching their desired haven and of coming to fertile land. However, it is probable that with the question of a pilot the Pilgrims had no more to do than with choosing the other officers of the ship, all of whom were furnished by their hard masters, the Merchant Adventurers.

That part of the coast first sighted was the best-known point between Nova Scotia and Florida. Eastern Massachusetts had already been explored by men of three nations, Samuel Champlain, John Smith, and Adrian Block, and visited by not a few fishermen, traders, and English slavers, or kidnapers, of Indians. Smith had in 1614 made a map, which these "humorists," as Smith called the Pilgrims, had taken instead of his advice. He had put a good many English names, fanciful and otherwise, upon his map, such as London, Cheviot Hills, Edinburgh, Cambridge, and so on, though some of these still hold their own, such as Plymouth, Charles River, and Cape Ann. Cape Cod was variously named: by Block, Flat Cape; by Smith, Cape James; and by later comers, Cape Malabar. Champlain had sprinkled some French names on his maps. Block, who rounded the cape and crossed to Nahant, and of whose fame Block Island is a monument, had given the name of Nassau to Buzzard's Bay, and others, now obliterated or anglicized, such as Rhode Island for Rood Eilandt. Housatonic is the Dutch Woesten Hoek or Wilderness Place. The Dutch claims were based on the right of discovery.

Had the Mayflower been steered due west, she would have reached the American coast at or near the place of John Cabot's landfall. There have been many theories, some ingenious, others absurd, as to why Cape Cod was made and held to. Most of the notions entertained are modern after-thoughts, and some are spawned out of disgraceful prejudices. Probably the real reason lay, not in the total depravity of the captain, or of the pilot, or of the Dutch, but in the Gulf Stream, that vast and shifting ocean current whose very existence was then unknown. As we now know, the channel of this river of indigo-blue warm water frequently changes, swerving miles east or west. Its vagaries could therefore easily puzzle even an experienced pilot, and drag the Mayflower northward. When Verrazzano set his compass for Florida, he also, and much to his surprise, made landfall at Cape Cod. Neither Jones, nor Coppin, nor the Dutch then knew anything of the Gulf Stream, which was first discovered and described by Dr. Benjamin Franklin.

Furthermore, like the French, and Captain John Smith, the English pilot had the idea, from which Englishmen were not wholly free till the eighteenth century, of finding gold mines or the mythical Indian city, called Norumbega. Quite probably this theory also had its influence in bringing the Mayflower to Cape Cod instead of Sandy Hook.

Geologists who have inquired concerning the ages past tell us that the eastern end of Massachusetts, shaped like an arm with an elbow and fist, was fashioned by the forces of glacier and floe-bergs, wind, ice, and waves. These hollowed out Boston Harbor, and ground and shaped its many islands, depositing the detritus in the form of a sandy hook or bar, which is now Barnstable County. Sandy Hook, named by the Dutch, is another instance of matter redeposited as a bar, after a bay has been scoured out.

It was at break of the day on the 10th of November that the shore was first spied. The sea-weary eyes of the passengers were comforted at "especially seeing so goodly a land, and wooded to the brink of the sea." It was probably to the northern extremity of the cape that they came. After deliberation among themselves and with Captain

Jones, they tacked about and resolved to stand for the southward. "But after they had sailed that course about half the day, they fell among dangerous shoals and roaring breakers [probably at the Pollock Rip], and they were so far intangled therewith, as they conceived themselves in great danger; and the wind shrinking upon them withal, they resolved to bear up again for the Cape; and thought themselves happy to get out of these dangers before night overtook them, as by God's good providence they did."

Evidently to these landsmen, crowded together almost like slaves in a slave vessel, poorly fed, enfeebled by their long confinement and bad air, barely escaping the dangers of foundering in the stormy mid-ocean, and now again in peril from treacherous shallows and currents which nearly caused shipwreck, it seemed in retrospect as though "a sea voyage was an inch of hell."

Furthermore the ship folk gave them clearly to understand that they must hurry up and get a place to settle, for the Mayflower would not stir from her good anchorage, and captain and crew were bound to keep enough victuals for themselves both while there and while on the way back to England. "Yea, it was muttered by some that if they got not a place in time, they would turn them and their goods ashore and leave them."

The Pilgrim Fathers having first been plain

farmers, and then mechanics in a strange country, and several times passengers by inland waters, salt sea, canal and ocean, now expected to become explorers, but "order is Heaven's *first* law." Before this work of spying out the land could begin, there was another question to settle, that of government.

They inherited the tradition of English freedom, but they had been nobly reinforced also by residence in a free republic, where the spirit of the churches was democratic and where that of the city and state was republican. They had seen before their own eyes in Holland what a large share the people had in the making of government. Above all, believing that even common men led by the spirit of God were kings and priests unto God, they had formed a little republic of their own. Their church life, theoretically democratic, was also practically so in large measure; though here, as in every form of social order on earth, the men of light and leading were powerful in influence, and able to overawe those of lesser ability, and move them for mutual good. Now that they were inside Cape Cod, instead of Sandy Hook, and their patent, which they had, conferred no rights in New England, since the Virginia Company had none there, the Mayflower was an "undocumented vessel" on the high seas. Furthermore there were symptoms of anarchy among some baser spirits in the party, which must be instantly met and curbed.

We must not forget that this Mayflower company was not the sifted and select party that had come from Leyden. There were a few people, as Bradford says, "shuffled" in upon them, who were probably unmitigated scoundrels. There were others also, hired laborers, who had not been trained and tempered in righteousness. These, so soon as the ship turned back from the southward, possibly, also, urged on by the sailors, were "not well affected to unity and concord," but "gave some appearance of faction." Between the two extremes — of foolishly indiscriminate laudation of "the one hundred and one" at banquets on Forefathers' Day, and Palfrey's dictum that "eleven (of the Pilgrims) are favorably known, the rest are either known unfavorably, or else only by name" — the truth probably lies midway.

Evidently, then, there was a necessity for some form of government, to be agreed upon, which the majority would adhere to and the minority must obey. So before undertaking exploration or anything on land, the men who had, according to the authority of the Bible, formed a church, — far better authority than popes or bishops or kings could give, — proceeded to form a government. This they had no difficulty in doing, for their "large patent" obtained for them by Sir Edwin Sandys permitted the leaders of "plantations" to make all necessary laws and forms of authority, provided they held loyally to the sovereign of England, and were not opposed to the laws of the realm. It was under this documented authorization that the Mayflower men elected, or rather confirmed, a governor and made the Cape Cod Compact, subscribing their names as subjects of the king of Great Britain. They formed themselves into a civil body politic for carrying out the purposes of planting a colony in the northern parts of Virginia. They promised all due submission to such just and equal laws as should be thought most meet and convenient for the general good.

The effective Mayflower company at Cape Cod consisted of seventy-three males and twenty-nine females. Of thirty-four adult males constituting the colony proper, eighteen had wives and fourteen of the eighteen had children under twenty-one, — twenty boys and eight girls. Of these thirty-four men, — the real nucleus of the colony, — probably all but four were from Leyden. But in addition to the householders and their heads, there was the uncertain element of servants, sailors, and craftsmen, large enough to be dangerous if not properly disposed and influenced. There was, indeed, in the Mayflower a majority of noble souls trained and tempered by long years of friendship and mutual joys and dangers. These, as Englishmen duly empowered by their charter, did what any sensible men of England,

Scotland, or Holland would have done at that time under like environment.

Thus, without looking at this document in the transfiguring glow of after-dinner oratory in later centuries, we may still see in it a noble framework of government, simple but efficient. It is not free from the stilted language and even the fictions of law which belong to the age. We read the phrase "dread sovereign lord," so common in those times, and we also find James called "the King of France," which, since the loss of Calais in January, 1558, was almost as ridiculous a term then as it would be now. It was sixty-two years behind the facts. As to King James being a "defender of the faith," this must have been to the Pilgrims a grim joke. The strong points of the document are, the sentences "in the name of God, Amen," and "having undertaken . . . to plant the first colony in the northern parts of Virginia; we do by these presents solemn and mutually in the presence of God and of one another covenant and combine ourselves together into a civil body politic." It was signed by forty-one men, out of the seventy-five male passengers then on board the Mayflower. Of the remaining twenty-four males, thirteen were sons and minors whose fathers' signatures answered for their own. Nine others who did not subscribe were male servants. These were probably too ill to sign or be interested in the matter, for all of them except one soon died, nor is it likely that they could write. This compact of the people, for the people, and by the people was expressed in a truly democratic document, and furnished the basis of one of the best governments that could be advised.

To the boys and girls, to say nothing of the adults, the first view of their new home was delightful. All around were the "trees of the Lord," such as those which they had seen in Holland and which had given that land of primeval forests its name. The ship lay inside the good harbor wherein a thousand sail of ships may safely anchor. They noticed that the timber came down to the water's edge; oaks, pine, juniper, and the sassafras, which was then esteemed extremely valuable in medicine, besides other sweet woods, could be discerned. So the first odors that greeted them were not of turf, or from burning hearth fires, — which to one approaching Ireland or England has such a suggestion of human habitations, — but the balsamic odors of the forest, of rude nature.

Now, also, they began to see their wretched poverty, how poorly they were prepared to make money or obtain food, or even to sustain life. There was the greatest store of fowl that they had ever seen. There were also whales, playing close to the ship, which, had they only possessed harpoons and ropes, they could have captured, and, trying out the oil, have secured what would now be sixty or eighty thousand dollars' worth of bone and oil. Whale-fleet, now "Wellfleet," still tells the story of past abundance. The Pilgrims tried to fish for cod, but found none, despite the name of the cape, for it was not the season. Indeed, all the time that the Mayflower lay there, seven weeks, they got no salt-water fish, but only a few little ones on the shore. They tried to eat the fat coarse mussels, but in their gastric condition such meat only made them ill.

They could not get nearer than three-quarters of a mile to the shore, for the waters were very shallow. When they sent sixteen armed men ashore to get firewood and fresh water, these had to wade through the freezing cold brine, because the anonymous shallop had been sagged out of shape by men sleeping in it during the voyage, and its seams were all opened. The sand hills were found to be much like the dunes of Holland, but with this difference, — that in many places below the overlying wind-blown sand lay excellent black earth, enriched by ages of growth and of fallen leaves and vegetable matter. The first product of the land which they used was juniper, or cedar wood, which they burned while on the ship, and it smelled very sweet and strong.

CHAPTER XV

IN THEIR THIRD HOME

After the Sabbath of November 23, practical life in the New World began on Monday, the 24th of November, by the women going ashore to wash clothes, which it had not been possible to do on board the ship, where all the fresh water in store was precious. We may imagine that the women had plenty to do, when they thus began the great American institution of "Wash-day Monday." They had been one hundred and thirty-three days on board ship since they left Delfshaven.

The "juniper," or red cedar, which made the aromatic fire under the wash kettles, has long since disappeared before the axe. The pool of fresh water, so useful for their laundry, is now submerged in Provincetown Harbor.

Thus began, also, in the cold raw air, the colds and coughs which put so many of them into their graves within a few weeks. One of the most pathetic facts about the first winter in their third home is the almost entire destruction of the wives of the Pilgrims, fourteen out of eighteen dying off, while four of the twenty-four households were entirely obliterated.

Meanwhile the stronger men were impatient to spy out the country, especially since there seemed to be a river opening into the main land. Miles Standish, the soldier, is now first mentioned in Pilgrim literature. He appears in view as captain of the exploring expedition, which was "rather permitted than approved." Of the sixteen picked men, all had swords and corselets. Their fire-arms were partly old-fashioned matchlocks, and partly "snaphances," which is a Dutch word for snap-cock guns. Their provisions were crackers and cheese, and their medicine a bottle of brandy. William Bradford, Stephen Hopkins, and Edward Tilley formed, with Standish, a council of advice.

The little company started off in single file, marching along the sea at the edge of the woods. Well used to ambuscades in the Netherlands, Standish was continually on the alert. After they had gone about a mile they saw the first human beings, five or six in number, with a dog. At first they supposed them to be the skipper and some of his crew, but soon saw that they were natives or Indians, who quickly ran away. Standish's party followed them for about ten miles, stepping in their trail, and losing sight of them after having seen them run up a hill, possibly Negro Head.

By this time night had come. Kindling a fire, they set two sentinels and slept on the ground. At break of day they resumed their march.

This time they went into the woods (which have long ago disappeared) through boughs and bushes, which damaged their armor lacings. They found no fresh water or food or Indian houses. At about ten o'clock they reached a deep valley marked with the little paths or tracks made by Indian feet, and there also they saw a deer and found springs. Heartily glad and long tired of the water kept in the ship's tanks, they sat down at or near what is now East Harbor, and drank fresh water with as much delight as ever they had drunk wine or beer in all their lives. Going southward they came to the shore of the bay and kindled a fire, as a signal to the Mayflower's people. After seeing a pond of fresh water, with many vines and wild fowl and much sassafras, they found about fifty acres of old maize-land which had been used by the Indians. Following the seashore awhile, and again moving inland, they saw Indian graves and a stubble field. Walnut-trees, strawberries, and grapevines were also noticed. The ruins of an old house, evidently the hut of European sailors, aroused their curiosity, for in it was a ship's kettle brought out of Europe, together with three or four bushels of corn, some of the ears of which were yellow, some red, and some mixed with blue. This maize with grains of various tints was a new and wonderful thing to these people, who had never, except perhaps in the Leyden museum, seen anything like it. While thus eagerly occupied, they were all, as on every occasion, very alert, posting sentinels in a ring.

At night they came back to the fresh-water pond, reared a barricade against the wind, and set a watch. The sentinels stood with matches burning all night long during the rain. Next morning as they further wandered, Bradford, the file-closer, was caught, but not hurt, in a deer trap, which some Indian had made by bending down a sapling held with a noose, strewing acorns underneath the trigger. No doubt Bradford's comrades had a hearty laugh over the mishap, out of which he got so easily. They scared up partridges, wild geese, and ducks, but bagged no game. They even saw three deer; and Bradford cracks a joke to the effect that one buck on the shoulder is worth three in the woods. When within sight of their ship they fired their guns, and the longboat came to fetch them back, and there was mutual gladness. The corn was held for seed, and the Indian noose made of wild hemp kept for imitation, both to be paid for, should the owners be found.

While the shallop was being repaired, time was spent in sawing timber, fashioning tool handles, and otherwise preparing for the making of homes. On Monday, the 27th of November, thirty-four men, including Captain Jones, the commander, and nine sailors, set out on a new expedition. It blew and snowed all day and night, so that some of the men "took the original of their death here." Sailing into the river which they had discovered, they found it was not navigable for ships. It must have been a delightful variation to their monotonous fare, when on the night of Tuesday they had three fat geese and six ducks for supper. These they ate with soldiers' appetites.

The next day, Wednesday, they left the hilly region and turned toward the Indian granary. By a lucky shot two geese were killed. Launching the Indian canoe, they crossed over, seven or eight at a time. Digging in Corn Hill they obtained about ten bushels of maize. The next day they came to a mound, which they dug open, finding two skeletons, of a man and of a child, wrapped up in bundles and packed in red powder. On the man's head was fine yellow hair. The child had strings of shells wrapped around the limbs, and there were toys near by. Whether, as has been supposed, this was the body of a Norseman, or whether the finely carved and painted board with fleur-de-lis upon it pointed to the loss on the coast, in 1616, of a French ship, is not known. The wreck would explain the numerous European relics found by the Pilgrims. It is known that one white survivor had married in the tribe and had had a son. The child was probably arrayed for burial by a sorrowing Indian mother. The

Pilgrims scrupulously covered up the grave-mound. They found also two empty wigwams, into which two sailors from the ship or shallop had also entered. In addition to the Indian baskets and implements, were deer's heads and hoofs, eagle claws, seeds, food, material to make mats, and a European bucket. To all these things the explorers helped themselves freely, intending to pay for them when they could. Toward night, December 10, they boarded the shallop and reached the ship.

After a long discussion as to their place of settlement, they decided not to seek another distant harbor, but to make some discovery within the bay, and there settle, as Coppin advised them to do. The number of males on the ship was increased by the birth of Peregrine (Pilgrim) White, who lived until the year 1704.

All this time, it must have been hard work to keep so many small boys out of mischief, nor was it entirely possible to do this, cooped up as they were on shipboard. On the 15th of December, Tuesday, young Francis Billington, while his father was away, had got hold of some gunpowder. Besides shooting off the musket once or twice, he made squibs, and enjoyed himself as the small boy loves to do with things dangerous. Not content with this, having found a loaded fowling piece, he discharged it in the cabin, where there was a little barrel of powder about half full, which had probably been opened to supply the cartridges or bandoleers of the explorers. Loose powder lay scattered about the cabin, and the fire from the muzzle was within four feet of the bunk, so that, with many flints and iron things lying around, where so many people were crowded together, it is a wonder that the ship was not blown up. Of this Billington boy and his pranks the company were to hear again.

A third exploring party, consisting of twelve Pilgrims and six of the crew, set out on the 16th of December in cold, hard weather. While the shallop was being rowed with exhausting labor clear of Long Point, two of the men became ill and one nearly swooned with cold. But once clear of the sandy point, they hoisted sail, caught the wind, and got into smoother water, though the spray froze on their clothes. After some hours they landed, made a barricade, built fires, and posted sentinels. Four or five miles off they saw the smoke of the Indians' fire. The next morning twelve explorers spent a fatiguing day on land, rejoining the shallop at dark. They were very hungry and very faint, but after a little food and warmth they went to sleep. At midnight they were alarmed by the crying of "foxes," as they thought, which were driven off by firing guns.

The next morning at five o'clock they tried their muskets. These men were of the sort that feared God and kept their powder dry. They had prayer, and after eating started again. Now came the first meeting between these men of iron and those still living in the stone age. Suddenly in the winter dawn they heard the same cry which had disturbed them at midnight. It was an Indian warwhoop. The next moment one of the men, being out from the camp, ran in, crying, "They are men, Indians, Indians!" and then a shower of arrows came flying among them. These missiles were tipped with deer horn, eagle claws, or brass. Fortunately none of the white men were hit, though the shafts came very close on every side, and some of their coats hung up on the barricade were shot through and through.

The whites ran to the beach to get their arms and armor. Captain Miles Standish had a snapcock gun, and he and a comrade fired. By this time Bradford and another man were ready, there being only four at that moment fit for combat, but Standish ordered them to withhold fire until they could take aim. It looked as if a battle were coming on. The men near the fire called to their comrades in the shallop, asking how it was, and heard three shots from them and a call for a firebrand to light their match cord. One of the men at the camp seized a burning fagot and rushed with it to the boat, to give the men a light. Meanwhile terrific Indian yells sounded in their ears. By this time all the company had got their arms. The Indian chief was behind a tree and let fly three arrows at short range, which the white men dodged or avoided by stooping down. The chief stood his ground even when some one fired three shots of a musket at him. On the fourth shot, the Indian yelled, and then all the red men fled. Warily leaving six men to keep the shallop, the Pilgrim squad pursued the savages for a quarter of a mile, but did not come up with them. It was supposed from the sound that there were thirty or forty warriors, but in the morning twilight they could not easily be seen among the trees, while on the other hand the white men were readily discerned by the light of the fire. They picked up eighteen of the arrows to be sent to England by the captain. Then they thanked God, took courage, and went on their journey, calling this place "The First Encounter." This battlefield was at Nauset, which Champlain had visited a few years before. It is now called Eastham, and the Indians were the Nausites. It seems wonderful that with so many arrows and bullets flying through the air no one was hurt.

The next day was snowy and rainy with high winds. The rudder hinges having broken, two men had to steer the boat with oars. The mast split in three pieces, and the danger was great. Late in the afternoon they found an island and a sandy place good for the shallop to ride safe and secure for the night, during which sentinels kept watch. As Clark, the captain's mate, was first to land, they named it Clark's Island.

On the 20th of December, it being the Sabbath, they rested. On Monday they sounded the harbor, which they found very good for their shipping, and then made the landing, possibly on the rock now so famous. They found close at hand maize fields, running streams, and a hill for defense — all the requisites for a successful settlement. This was the scene of their future home, "a place very good for situation." It was no other than the place named Plymouth by Captain John Smith. This is the date of "Forefathers' Day," which began to be annually celebrated in 1769.

The next day, Tuesday, they made straight for the ship, carrying the good news to their people, who were greatly comforted. On the 25th of December the Mayflower hoisted anchor to make the run across the bay to Plymouth; but unable to do so on account of contrary winds, she put back again towards Cape Cod. On Saturday, the 26th, the wind being fair, they came safely into Plymouth Harbor. Other visits on shore and explorations were made, and it was shown that here was a good site, rich in all kinds of sea food, with abundance and variety of timber and herbs, and having a fairly fertile soil.

After calling on God for guidance, the final council was held on the morning of Wednesday, December 30. They decided by a majority vote to settle at Plymouth, where there were cleared land, plenty of fresh water, a hill on which a fort could be built and made, like the Burg at Leyden, a place whence to view the surrounding country.

The Pilgrim settlement was in a certain respect copied after that in Leyden. The company was arranged into households, the single men being required to join some family, so that fewer houses might be required. Not given at this time to mere words or much sentiment, they laid out a nameless thoroughfare, first called "The Street," then "First Street," "Broad Street" (the name of the main street in Leyden), and finally, in 1823, "Leyden Street." In their housekeeping they were crowded together, as they had been in the city on the Rhine, in their little houses, every one of which contained probably an average of ten persons.

Troubled and discouraged with rain and wet, storm and snow, they kept on at work, during the dark days of late December and the increasing cold of early January, losing much time in going and coming between ship and shore, for the tide waited not for their convenience, and the Mayflower lay nearly a mile and a half away. They had no time to make shingles or to bake tiles, such as they lived under in Leyden, so on the 13th of January parties went out to gather thatch wherewith to put something between themselves and the sky. As yet only a few of the men had seen any human being. Not having any small fish-hooks, they caught no fish, and the finding of a live herring on the shore was a great event. On Monday, the 18th of January, the shallop was sent out, coming back with three seals and a cod-fish. On the same day one of the Billingtons, having climbed a high tree on a high hill, saw a sheet of water. Walking with one of the master's mates, he discovered "Billington Sea," from which the town brook issues.

The idea of calling a pond a "sea" is old English, and the use of the word is illustrated in the "sea" of Galilee, as Lake Gennesaret is called. This was among the first seen of the two hundred ponds which lie in Plymouth township, but it was not the source of the Hudson River, as probably some of the company then supposed. Even until near the time of the Revolution, New England was supposed by many in Great Britain to be an island. It was so referred to even by one of King George's high officers.

CHAPTER XVI

THE FIRST FAMILIES OF AMERICA

On the 19th of January, the weather being reasonably fair, the town was laid out, and the plots of ground were assigned. The big common house, which was to be a rendezvous, church, barracks, hospital, and storehouse, was twenty feet square, made of hewn logs, pointed with mortar or mud in the chinks between the timbers, and thatched. The work was slow, for the winter days were short, and the rains often made them stop. On Friday, the 22d, two men, having gone out for thatching material, followed too far their dogs that chased the deer, and lost their way in the woods. They had no arms except a sickle. They had to make their bed on the ground, and were kept awake by the roaring of wolves. They walked up and down under a tree all the night, which was extremely cold, expecting to climb up in the branches when the wolves came, though these failed to appear. By the next night they reached the company, nearly dead with hunger and cold.

As we have seen, there were no "Tylers" in the party, but only "Thatchers." Very probably, these Leyden people had not been used to thatch and its dangers. We know not what sort of a chimney these amateur house-builders had erected, or whether there was any; but the roof of the big common house caught on fire. A spark flew up into the thatch, which burst into flame, making a tremendous blaze. Seen from the ship, the people on board supposed that the Indians had attacked and burned the place. The house was full of bedding. The guns were loaded, with powder near at hand. Carver and Bradford lay sick at the time, but fortunately they got up quickly and saved themselves and the building from an explosion.

Three or four days of sunshine followed, and then more rain, but by the 30th a shed was built to shelter the goods of the community, which were now brought over from the ship. On Sunday, January 31, the whole company, being ashore, met for divine service in the common house,—New England's first public building. Local tradition declares that Mary Chilton was the first woman who stepped on land, and that for her and the others the solitary boulder was the landing-place. Plymouth Rock began with her its fame.

On the 14th of February a most tremendous storm burst upon them. It knocked the mud out of the chinks in the houses, and made the Mayflower rock in a lively way, for she was now empty of her lading and unballasted. Again, the house being full of sick people, they were in danger from a fire kindled by a spark, though no great harm was done. Probably too much birch fuel was used. Captain Jones, having killed five geese, distributed them among the sick.

The Indians now appeared, off and on, in such numbers that it was necessary to be prepared with some kind of defensive organization. So, on Saturday, the 27th of February, 1621, a meeting was called to form a military company. Miles Standish was made captain, and given authority to command. In the fort the Pilgrim battery consisted of four cannon. Hard as must have been the work of landing the artillery, it must have been harder to drag the two light and two heavy pieces up to the top of the hill, where they were to be planted in a commanding situation. The sailors, however, lent a hand, and reinforced Pilgrim muscle.

Evidently not knowing the New England climate, they had begun to sow some garden seeds on the 7th of March. On the 13th of March they heard thunder for the first time in their new homeland. Friday, March 26, 1621, was a fair, warm day. While busy with further council about military affairs, there came a sudden and delightful interruption. They heard their own native tongue uttered by a savage, who said "Welcome." He was naked, except a fringe of skin about his waist, and had a bow and two arrows.

He was tall and straight, with his black hair hanging down behind him, and cut on his forehead like a bang, and was entirely beardless. He asked for beer, but they gave him brandy and some biscuit and butter, cheese and pudding, and a piece of mallard duck, all of which he was well accustomed to, and liked very much.

This Indian gentleman, for such we must call him, being, as he was, from one of the first families of America, and by name Samoset, was also a man of culture and travel. He was a chief, a native of Pemaquid, where Bristol, Maine, now stands. Having come on Captain Dermer's ship with another countryman named Squanto, he landed on Cape Cod, where six French fishermen had been shipwrecked only six months before the Mayflower arrived. Samoset helped to redeem two survivors from their savage captors, and probably told of that Frenchman from an earlier wreck, who, with his half-breed child, had filled the grave which the Pilgrim explorers opened. Instead of going back home, Samoset had remained in this region, and was now able to tell the Pilgrims the history of the land they were to live on, and why the Indians were so hostile. English slave-traders had in 1614 kidnaped and sold into the Spanish galleys twenty-seven natives. Hence the red man's desire for revenge upon all whites. The Pilgrims' tenure of land was not likely to be disputed, for there were no other claimants.

About four years before, a plague had swept off all the people in the neighborhood, which was called Patuxet. The nearest chief was Massasoit.

When on Saturday Samoset left, he was given a knife, a bracelet, and a ring. He promised to return within a night or two, and to bring with him some of Massasoit's men, with such beaver-skins as they had for barter.

Samoset came back with most undesirable promptness on Sunday. With him were five sturdy Indians, whose bodies and legs were more or less covered with deer and panther skin. Since the Pilgrims wore short, baggy trousers, with stockings coming to the knees, the Indian leggings seemed to them like "Irish trousers," coming all the way up to the thighs and waist. In complexion they resembled the gypsies, whom the Plymouth men had seen in England and Holland. They had no hair on their faces, which were painted according to whim or fashion. The coarse black hair on their heads was braided into long tresses, banged on their foreheads, or tied up over their heads, with a feather or a fox tail hanging out. In token of peace, they had left their bows and arrows a quarter of a mile from the town. They ate heartily of the food offered them. They gave a specimen of their songs and dances. They carried at the waist their rations, — some powdered corn in a bag, — and their luxuries, which were pipes and a tobacco pouch. They brought back the tools taken in the woods, where the white men had left them. They had three or four skins for sale; but after proper politeness shown, it being Sunday, the Pilgrims drove no bargain, but got their red friends off. Samoset remained, and was furnished with a hat, a pair of stockings, shoes, a shirt, and a piece of stuff for a loin cloth.

On three different occasions, while elaborating their military business, the Pilgrims had been interrupted by the coming of the strange people whom they were most likely to meet in combat. Again a squad of Indians approached, this time apparently whetting their arrows, and rubbing their bow-strings as if in defiance; but when four of the white men went over the Town Brook toward them, they ran away. It was on this day, March 31, that the last of the company finally left the Mayflower. The carpenter, who had been sick for a long time of the scurvy, fitted up the shallop, and brought all ashore. No doubt the actual prosaic facts of the landing and the subsequent fancies of poet and painter do not tally.

The next day, April 1, was also eventful, for while at public council they were again visited by Samoset, who this time was accompanied by Squanto, the only survivor of the Patuxet captives that had been kidnaped and carried away into slavery by Captain Hunt in 1614. Squanto had been in London, where he lived with Master John Slaney in Cornhill, and could therefore speak a little English. Besides bringing a few skins to sell and some dried red herring, the pair intimated that Massasoit and all his company were coming, and, indeed, were near at hand. That this was true, was soon proved. In about an hour they saw on the top of a hill a band of about sixty natives led by Massasoit. The whites chose Edward Winslow, who was the diplomatist of the company, to signify that they wanted peace and trade, and that they would confer with delegates sent by the Indians. The presents sent consisted of a knife and a copper chain with a jewel in it for Massasoit, an ear jewel for his brother Quadequina, and a pot of brandy, plenty of biscuit, and some butter for the party.

To these men of the stone age, Winslow made a speech in the name of King James, and the interpreters turned it into Algonquin as well as they were able. After Massasoit had eaten and drunk, he wanted to buy Winslow's armor and sword, which the owner would not sell. Feeling in good humor after his dinner, Massasoit left Winslow as hostage in custody of Quadequina, and with twenty unarmed men came over the Town Brook. There he was met by Captain Standish and Allerton, with half a dozen men, who escorted him to an unfinished house, where they placed a rug and cushions. Governor John

Carver, with drummer, trumpeter, and a few men in armor, came in also. After salutations, Carver called for brandy and drank to Massasoit's health, while the red man also drained a "bumper." "The king" and his followers were also given fresh meat. Then followed a treaty of peace, which lasted many years. The reds and the whites, the men of stone and the men of iron, savage and Christian, mutually agreed not to injure or hurt each other, and to be friends and allies in war and peace.

Squanto, who remained a little while longer, made himself very useful to these Englishmen, who knew next to nothing about maize or its nature. He showed them how to plant the chief American staple, by first manuring the ground with fish, putting the grain and the alewives in the same hill. He further showed them how to hoe the earth around the stalks to secure fat ears. By the middle of April, he said, there would be plenty of fish coming up the Town Brook, and he also told them where to get other provisions. In due time the whites found by their own trial and experience that what Squanto had told them was true. He also taught them just how to catch eels. Going out on the muddy shore and treading them out with his feet, he caught a mess. Thus, without a trap, hook, or net, he provided sea food offhand. These eels were fat, sweet, and very nutritious. In many other helpful ways the red men were teachers and benefactors of the foreigners. Moccasins, snow-shoes, birch-bark canoes, and the art of "girdling" trees and thus quickly opening forest-land to sunshine and cultivation, were the great gifts of the Indians.

It was proper for the Plymouth men to return the call of Massasoit, to learn more about the country and to continue the league of peace. For this purpose Governor Carver chose Stephen Hopkins and Edward Winslow to go among them. Squanto, as the official interpreter, was presented with a bright red cotton coat, properly laced. This was not a military sign, for the red-coated soldier of the British army was not known until after the days of the Commonwealth. The embassy started on Monday, July 2, at nine in the morning, but did not meet Massasoit until far inland, on Wednesday, the 14th of July. The chief promised to continue peace and friendship and to procure good seed corn for them. Then they all lighted their pipes and talked of England and King James, who at this time had no wife, and of the Frenchmen who came often to Narragansett. When they went to bed, which they did without any supper, the chief and his squaw lay at one end of the couch, which was made of plank with a thin mat upon it. Two more of the Indians, for want of room, also pressed by and upon the Englishmen so that they were worse of their lodging than of their journey. The next day the Indians entertained them at games, and the white men shot at a mark, using "hail," or bird-shot, which made the Indians wonder to see the target so full of holes. At about one o'clock that day, two fish, probably bass, shot with arrows, were brought in and boiled, and out of this meal forty men took their sustenance.

By this time the white men had had enough of life in the stone age. They had not enjoyed deep slumbers, for the barbarous noises by which the Indians sang themselves to sleep, the vermin inside the wigwam, and the mosquitoes outside allowed them very little rest. Longing for a quiet Sabbath at home, they set out on Friday, Massasoit being both grieved and ashamed that he could not better entertain them. Having to subsist on such nourishment as they could gather by the way, they wrote on to Plymouth, sending the letter by Indian messengers, asking that food be sent them to Amasket. Wet, weary, and footsore they reached home on Saturday.

The next adventure was a voyage made by ten men of the company to find the small boy, John Billington, Jr., who had strayed off at the end of July and wandered up and down some five days, living on berries and what he could find. After much travel and trouble they found and brought him back. Other adventures among the Indians were in the form of an expedition to chastise the enemies of Massasoit at Namaschet, where there was some fighting, though no one was killed, and an expedition to Boston Bay, where they made a treaty of peace with the natives there. These were of the Massachusetts tribe, who took their name from a "hill shaped like an arrow-head," probably the Blue Hills near Boston.

Indian life then, as it had been for centuries previous, was one monotonous story of war, of human beasts seeking their prey, of fighting and murder, the savages finding such food as they could, and from time to time being swept off by contagious diseases.

CHAPTER XVII

SICKNESS AND HEALTH, WAR AND DIPLOMACY

THAT first winter of the Pilgrims at Plymouth was the most doleful in all their history. Starting out from Leyden with the young, strong, and healthy, their augmented numbers at Southampton had been sifted at Plymouth, and none had died on the voyage except young William Button. Why, then, were both the colonists and the Mayflower crew so frightfully decimated again and again?

When we consider the crowded ship's cabins, the hatches battened down, and the people kept over two months without proper ventilation or possible cleanliness, and the five weeks' exposure in midwinter on ship and shore at Cape Cod, there is no mystery. Many on board the ship were already reduced by scurvy. The food was bad and with little variety, and in those days the salt used was impure and often much more fit for paving material than for food. The first house built immediately became a hospital, "as full of beds as they could lie one by another," — the same bedding which had already been used in the ship. Nearly every person, at one time or another, was ill, and one half of the company died of quick consumption.

When the landspeople were through with their worst misery, the shipfolk inhabiting their germ-infested quarters were taken with the same epidemic. "The disease began to fall among the seamen, so as almost half their number died before they went away." One half of the whole human freight of the Mayflower found graves in earth or water before the return of the ship, on the 15th of April, 1621.

On land the deaths in December numbered six, in January eight, in February seventeen, in March thirteen, and during the rest of the year, six more. There is significance in the ages of those who died. Of thirty-six out of the sixty-one adult Pilgrims, most were between the ages of twenty and thirty, when the liability to pulmonary consumption is greatest. Only seven out of the thirty-two youths and children, but eight out of the nine servants, died. In a word, what killed off the Pilgrims during the first year was the infectious disease, acute pulmonary tuberculosis, or "galloping consumption." From that day until this, consumption has ever been the scourge of New England, and the greatest single cause of death among adults in the Eastern States. The emigrants who survived disease and exposure were undoubtedly tough. They made splendid stock for the building up of families and the state.

Governor Carver, in April, 1621, worn out with many labors in three countries and on the sea, as counselor, agent, nurse, farmer, magistrate, and man of God, was stricken in the field and died, after but a few hours of distress. He was buried with such official honors as the little band could render. Before summer was ended, the body of his devoted wife was laid by his side in the earth. As in the case of the other dead, the heroic survivors dared not mark the spots, lest savage enemies might count the graves. William Bradford was then chosen governor. With the exception of five years, when he refused reappointment, he served in this office until his death in 1657.

Rheumatism, sciatica, and scurvy, at first, and later, smallpox, troubled the colonists; but from one disease, common in Old and New England, the Pilgrim company was wholly free. This was the "bewitchment sickness." The medical books of those days show that physicians and common people believed that there were "pinings and wastings of the whole body, which many times so altered it as if it was not the same creature, causing various and foolish actions, in which many have called their children changelings, the alteration in their outward form, as well as of the mind, has been so great." It was then part of popular and even learned theology, and of medical "science," that the devil took up his residence in the human body and made it his playground. Many remedies were enumerated which were supposed to be "offensive to devils," such as mistletoe, ivy, coral, peony, rue, loadstone, amber, and various jewels. One or more of these antidotes to witchcraft were worn about the body by thousands of people in Europe. Cinnabar, put into a goosequill, or into a hazelnut, sealed up with wax, was good to hang on the pit of the stomach. A ring made of an ass's hoof was also recommended. Children were to be removed from the company of the supposed witch, in order that the influences which caused this disease of fascination might be neutralized.

In those days, when medicine was more mixed up with astrology, and theology with superstition, than now, and when thousands of people were judicially put to death, often by burning, for sorcery and witchcraft, it is certainly remarkable, though not inscrutable, that the Pilgrims had no epidemic of witchcraft. This was not because all the people of Plymouth, in the second generation, at least, did not believe in witches, for many of them shared the common notions of the times, — that human beings actually had direct dealings with the devil, — and late in their history they embodied this superstition in their laws. There were even two trials for witchcraft, within the Old Colony, but with this remarkable difference, as compared with those in Salem, — they cross-examined the witnesses, scanned their testimony, and found the charges not proved.

In a word, the Plymouth men were Europeans who had been born or educated and trained in the Dutch republic, where, during the very year that France, Germany, and England were putting to death thousands of people accused of witchcraft, was heard the first modern voice to rebuke this insanity of the human mind. After John Wier, of Grave, in 1563 challenged the very existence of witches, came a long line of writers ending with Balthazar Bekker, who in his classic work, "The Bewitched World," gave the final death blow to the superstition by exposing the worthlessness of the theory upon which it was founded. Long before the Pilgrims had arrived in Leyden, Holland was bathed in an atmosphere of wholesome skepticism, and the Leyden church thrived in the tonic air. Bekker was a benefactor of the human race. After his book, witchcraft took its place with the moles and the bats.

This remarkable state of affairs in their second home, when accusations of witchcraft and witch trials were at their height in their first homeland, must have powerfully impressed the Pilgrims dwelling in Leyden, and so the new world to which they came was not one bewitched. The Pilgrims showed themselves proof against this superstition. When the madness fell upon the Salem community, smiting wise and foolish alike, the Plymouth people were cooler-headed, and showed handsomely the results of their training in the land which an English Jubilee poet, in 1897, salutes as the "First Home of Mental Liberty."

The first crops did fairly well. Although the peas blossomed, they were parched in the sun and not worth gathering, but the maize proved to be then, as it is now, the most important American crop.

Happy over their first harvest, Governor Bradford sent men to go out and shoot some wild fowl, that they might have, not one Thanksgiving Day, but a whole week of fun, frolic, rejoicing, and gratitude to God. These hunters in one day killed so much feathered game as would, with side dishes, supply the company of about fifty survivors almost a week. This season, which may have been early in October, is sometimes called the beginning of our national American Thanksgiving Day, though at Plymouth, so far as we know, this first festival had no special religious features, certainly not so definitely as the historic day of October 3, which they had for ten years seen celebrated in Leyden. The Pilgrims began every day with prayer and thanksgiving, and enjoyed their religion on no particular day, but on all of them. They observed a perpetual joyful Sabbath. They were religious in everything, whether in eating, drinking, or working, in their pleasures as well as their duties and devotions.

What they wanted now, after harvest toil, was mirth and frolic, recreation and feasting; and so, inviting the Indians to come and enjoy the gladsome season, they "exercised their arms" — no doubt shooting at a mark, bows and arrows contending with muskets and ball at the ranges. In other words, they enjoyed one of the Doelen or target festivals, such as they had so often seen in Holland as well as in England. We can easily picture these men in corselets and bandoleers, top hats and knee breeches, firing their heavy guns from a rest, while the red archers used the most ancient of all long-range weapons. What a tremendous impulse has been given to civilization by gunpowder! What an evolution from the stone chip to the finished leaden arrow — the fulminate copper cartridge!

The Indians who came with Massasoit numbered about ninety men, and these also were feasted and entertained during three days. The red men themselves provided much of the fare, having gone out and killed five deer, the choice pieces of which they gave to Governor Bradford, Captain Standish, and others. It was true statesmanship for the Pilgrim leaders thus to win so soon the good will of the natives, and the fruits of their excellent Indian policy were already apparent, for they could "walk as peaceably and safely in the woods as in the highways in England." Evidently these men, long used to town life, had not yet become skillful enough to hunt deer very successfully, and so they appreciated all the more the friendliness of the Indians in bringing venison.

By the time that the first anniversary of their arrival had come round, seven dwellings had been completed, besides four houses for the use of the community. Others were in preparation. The climate at first seemed much like that of England, except that the summers were hotter; the winter was no colder, though they found later that the season of 1620–21 had been a mild one. Fish and fowl were in great abundance, the cod coming in the summer and being but "as coarse meat" with them. This "Cape Cod turkey," which has for centuries filled the stomachs and enriched the brains of dwellers in the Eastern States, is a fish that can be cooked in manifold ways, eaten salt or fresh, is good all the year round, and is easily preserved. The codfish is nature's great gift to Massachusetts. Bradford probably did not then foresee that what the wool sack was to England — the emblem of its wealth, and in honor made the chief seat in Parliament — the codfish would be to Massachusetts, and in gilded effigy hang in the chief legislative hall beneath a golden dome under which his own precious manuscript would rest in the year of grace 1897.

Besides the bay's being full of lobsters, a hogshead of eels, dug out of their beds, could often be taken in a night with small labor. All winter there were mussels and clams at their doors, and the Indians also brought oysters. Good solid herbs sprang up naturally in the springtime, with strawberries, gooseberries, grapes, and plums of various hue and species. Bradford was delighted at the great abundance of roses, which though single were very sweet indeed. He also noted other flowers, and the curious noises, particularly those of mosquitoes, seventeen-year locusts, and rattlesnakes. The country wanted only industrious men to cultivate it; and from over-crowded England such men ought to come. Even in winter, when no farming could be done, the women kept busy in household work and in making and mending clothing, while the men cut timber, made clapboards, stripped off sassafras, bought furs, and stored up a cargo to send to Europe at the first opportunity.

When on the 19th of November, 1621, Indian runners from Cape Cod informed them that a ship was at hand, which they thought to be French, it being too early to expect a friendly vessel, Bradford ordered the cannon to be fired to call home the men in the fields and assemble the little army of twenty men. Whereupon, every man and boy that could handle a gun stood to arms. Happily, instead of a man-of-war full of preying enemies, in sailed a ship smaller even than the Speedwell with praying Christians from Leyden. All on board were in good health, having suffered, during their long passage of four months, nothing more than seasickness. The first night after landing, a son was born of goodwife Ford. This ship, the Fortune, of fifty-five tons, or one fourth the size of an Erie canal-boat, brought thirty-five persons. These were mostly young men, more lively than foresighted, and with good appetites. Not having much provision left, they had to be satisfied with what the Pilgrims could offer them out of their own store. The sight of the toil-worn and partly ragged colonists removed any rosy illusions which the newcomers may have had. New England was not yet a land of luxury.

The Mayflower had gone back empty, because the colonists had not time or opportunity to load a cargo. The Fortune, on the contrary, was laden with beaver skins and other peltry, with sassafras, prepared timber, and clapboards, worth in all about five hundred pounds, or, appraised in money of our day, ten thousand dollars. John Alden, the cooper, would oversee the clapboards, and Dr. Fuller the sassafras.

Though returning rich as a fat sheep, the Fortune was destined to illustrate the proverb of going for wool and coming home shorn. She sailed away on December 23; but belying her "hail," this little craft, — no wonder the Bible revisers of 1611 called a fishing-smack on the "sea" of Galilee a "ship," — when near the English coast, January 29, 1622, was captured by a French man-of-war and taken to God's Island (Isle Dieu). The cargo was confiscated by the French governor, and the company of thirteen persons, after imprisonment and rough treatment, were only too glad to get away from Isle Dieu to "God's country," England. Their captor compelled them to sign a paper, saying that he had taken only two hogsheads of "fox" skins. Being ignorant of beaver and not expert in zoölogy, the Frenchman gave the best name he could think of to the animal which was destined to be the financial salvation of the colony, and to adorn the flag of colonial New York, the arms of more than one American city and state, and the Continental money of the Revolution. What the Frenchmen did with this English vessel, however, was nothing more than what Englishmen and Spaniards, Dutchmen and Danes very frequently did to each other. The law of the safety of the seas, which is now that of the civilized world, was in process of evolution, and Hugo de Groot's great book on international law was not yet written.

After the Fortune's misfortune, Canonicus, chief of the Narragansetts, evidently felt inclined to move out on the warpath. He sent a messenger to Plymouth with a bundle of new arrows wrapped in rattlesnake skin.

When Squanto returned and saw the Indian substitute for a letter and heard how the messenger had acted, he translated the emblem as meaning a challenge. It was the Indian's way of flinging down the gauntlet. The serpent skin and the arrows were as real a symbol of war as the caduceus of Mercury is of commerce, or the dove and olive leaf are of peace. After some deliberation, Governor Bradford stuffed the skin full of powder and shot and returned the document. At this answer of defiance to the savages, their "king" was terrified, and would not touch it or have it stay in his house or country. Indeed, all the Indians were far more afraid of the dead skin than if it had life within it, with sounding rattles at one end and lidless eyes and poison fangs at the other. They posted it from place to place, and at length the skin, with its novel stuffing, came back whole to Plymouth.

These Plymouth men were neither bullies nor cowards. They offered prayer and employed the wisest and best means, that their prayers might be answered. So ever looking to the Great Friend of Man, even while using their reason and having as yet no other defenses than their arms, they began to build palisades around the little town. They hewed down young trees, and, cutting off the branches, set their ends well in the ground and braced them at the top. By hard work throughout the month of February and a few days in March, they were able to have a wall for their dwellings. The little town nestled at the foot of what is now Burial Hill, and the palisades ran up the slope from the town to the fort. There were also four bastions, in three of which were gateways. Miles Standish commanded the military band, which was also organized and trained to act as a fire company.

During the two years, 1621 and 1622, these Plymouth people lived in a state of semi-famine. During four months of the latter year, having no bread, they were forced to live out of the sea on clams and fish, with an occasional bit of game from the woods and groundnuts. They had even to feed new immigrants who came without provisions, such as the six or seven who arrived on the fishing-fleet, in May, 1622, by way of Maine, and also the Weymouth party of fifty or sixty sent by Weston in the ships Charity and Swan. During this winter they tried once more, but in vain, to double Cape Cod and get by sea southward; and Squanto, who had encouraged them to do so, died. They made a trip to Boston Bay, finding trade very poor. At Nauset they secured, but only after great toil, eight or ten hogsheads of corn and beans.

Occasionally a little cheer lightened their dark days. When an Indian stole some beads and scissors from the shallop while lying in a creek, Standish went to Aspinet, the sachem, and demanded the return of the goods or the culprit. The doughty captain took leave, refusing gifts or kindness. The next morning Aspinet came to make up, and in such a comical way that the white men could hardly keep from laughter. The Indian chief thrust out his tongue, so that one could see its very root, and licked the captain's hand from the wrist to the finger's end, — evidently an imitation of a dog's way of making an apology. Then, following a fashion imitated from the English, having been taught by Squanto, he got down on his marrow bones, but in so rude and savage a manner as to bring a smile to the white men's faces. After that he handed back the beads to Captain Standish, assuring him that he had flogged the thief and had made the women bake bread for the white men. It was all as amusing as if in a comic opera.

The wolf being still at the door and starvation more than a possibility, Bradford went to the two other places, Middleboro and Sandwich, to buy corn. The "noble" red man, in a state of nature, makes his wife a beast of burden. In a state of grace he at least helps her. From the former place, the grain was transported upon the backs of the squaws, who were taken ill on the road, so that the Plymouth men had to go after the food and bring it home. At another time, being still uncertain whether they would not yet die of starvation, Captain Standish, in the bitter winter weather, went with the shallop to Barnstable Harbor for more food, and got it through vigilance rather than violence. Being obliged to lodge in the wigwam on account of the great cold, "God possessed the heart of the captain with just jealousy," and while some of his company slept, others kept awake. When the Indians stole the beads Standish called up all his men and demanded satisfaction of the sachem. This so daunted the courage of the savages that they not only returned the beads, but brought out plenty of corn for trade and attempted no further injury.

Hearing that Massasoit was very ill and likely to die, and that a Dutch ship had grounded on the beach near the chief's wigwam at Pokonokat, Bradford sent Winslow, who knew Dutch well, with John Hamden and the Indian Hobomok. Winslow was not only a good diplomatist, but had some skill in healing and nursing. He found that the ship had sailed away, but under his care Massasoit recovered.

Massasoit, in gratitude, had revealed to Winslow a plot of the Massachusetts Indians to kill all the Plymouth people. In a council of war, Standish and a picked band of eight men were authorized to go forth and bring back the head of Wituwamut, the ringleader, who was a bold and bloody villain. Arriving in the Indian country, this committee of justice were not able to get many of the red men together; but Standish and four comrades, finding themselves in a wigwam with Pecksuwot, Wituwamut, and another young brave, the captain gave the signal and a fearful struggle began. The three Indians were killed, another, a youth, was hanged, and in all seven red men were slain and the plot came to naught.

The medicine administered by Standish was drastic but salutary. The other savages were struck with terror. "They forsook their houses, running to and fro like men distracted, living in swamps and other places, and so brought manifold diseases amongst themselves whereof many are dead." The head of Wituwamut was stuck upon one of the palisades of the fort. It was then a general European custom to expose the heads of criminals, just as it was in Japan in 1870, as I have often seen. Much later in the colony's history, the head of "King Philip" was exposed upon the fort in a similar manner for over twenty years. Something as wonderful as the swarm of honey-making bees in the skeleton of the lion slain by Samson entered. A pair of wrens made their nest in the skull.

The summer of 1623 was a very discouraging one, for although the colonists worked hard in preparing the soil and sowing the seed, there was a great drought, during six weeks of which there was hardly any rain ; but showers at last fell and saved their crops. In the spring also, a Scotsman named David Thompson, who had begun a plantation at Portsmouth, New Hampshire, sold some food to Captain Standish and returned with him to visit Plymouth.

At about the beginning of August two vessels, the ship Ann, of one hundred and forty tons, and the Little James, a pinnace of forty-four tons, came with provisions, bringing about one hundred new colonists, who found no one sick at Plymouth and none dead since the woeful winter of 1621. Many of the newcomers were old friends from Leyden, including near and dear relatives, and some had been passengers on the Paragon who had failed to get over on this unfortunate ship. A few others, however, who had been picked up by the Adventurers, were so plainly unfit for colonial life that Governor Bradford shipped them back to Europe at the expense of the Plymouth community. Thus was begun the American system of protection against pauperism, of which Castle Garden is in our day the exponent. The Pilgrim fleet had thus far brought about two hundred and thirty-three colonists.

The ship Little James, which had been built for the Adventurers, was fitted for trade and discovery to the southward, but proved an expensive and troublesome charge. The Ann set sail on the 20th of September, loaded with clapboards and peltry for England, where the demand for kegs for beer and fur for coats was great.

Edward Winslow returned to England in the Ann, and when at home wrote a book, which was printed in 1624, entitled "Good News from New England." He showed "three things that overthrow and bane plantations," and he described the religion of the natives, who groped after God if haply they might find him. It is interesting to compare, as landmarks of Christianity, Winslow's narrative and Whittier's "The Grave by the Lakeside." Thus, already, the Pilgrims were "in print" and well known to many interested persons. Winslow's book shows that in the building of their commonwealth they set the greatest store on character. Between their story and their glory, however, there is a difference. The first never lacked publicity from this year 1624. The latter has come more slowly.

While in England, though not until 1651, in his fifty-seventh year, Winslow had his portrait painted, and this, with Cuyp's picture of the Delfshaven exodus, makes two contemporary memorials in art. If the reputed portrait of John Carver be genuine, we have three.

CHAPTER XVIII

POLITICS: DOMESTIC AND FOREIGN

THE planting season of 1623 called for a new departure. Until this time the system had of necessity been coöperative, almost to communism, for the Pilgrims worked as a company rather than as individuals. This led to dissatisfaction, and ended in failure. In 1623 the land was divided and assigned, so that each person should have one acre, the division being according to lot.

At once there was a marked difference for the better. More land was planted, and all worked with new vigor, even the women and children going out gladly to help in the fields. Diplomacy was needed in dealing with the new people who had come over on the Little James, and who wanted to set up a separate colony. Conference and concession were necessary before there was perfect harmony between these new "Particulars" and the old "Generals." Early in 1624, of the two hundred and thirty-three persons who had arrived on the four ships, one hundred and eighty were living.

What kind of a government could these Plymouth men, ignored by their sovereign and living in a wilderness, form? Under what social and political methods could they live? In natural history a cultivated plant or animal which has been long accustomed to a special environment maintained under certain conditions, artificial or natural, usually "reverts" to a simpler type when the environment is changed or the previous conditions are removed. Whether strawberry or pigeon or man, this is the law. So these English people adopted the forms of life under which their ancestors had lived a thousand years previously. In Friesland and adjoining islands, these old Teutonic forms were still a living reality when the Plymouth men began their community at the edge of the American wilderness. The Pilgrims proceeded exactly as the Swiss democracies still do, and as I have seen them do, in their town meetings. Nearly everything was decided in general meeting of the whole colony. Outwardly, also, in the arrangement and apportionment of hogs and cattle, in their daily call by sound of the horn to common pasture, and in their going and coming at morning and evening, there was a marked resemblance to an ancient Teutonic village.

Nevertheless, in every form and under all forms of government, as I have noted, — in the despotism of Old Japan, or the freedom of the American commonwealth, in the ultra-democracy of a Congregational church or of a New England village, —

the zealous and willing men of superior intelligence, experience, character, and power influence and lead the others. There may be dummies on the thrones of despotism, and there may be popes and shahs in a democracy.

At first everything at Plymouth was decided after council, and then carried out by the governor. It was "Raad voor daad," as the Dutch say — Council before action; but late in 1623 the colonial records begin, and these show a government gradually but increasingly representative and delegated. Trial was by jury, and in an election all the males of the colony were entitled to take part if of full age. Though Bradford heartily believed in rotation in office, he was elected and reëlected many times. Edward Winslow served three years, Thomas Prence two years, Josiah Winslow one year, and Thomas Hinckley five years in the chief magistracy of Plymouth, before the tyranny of Andros trampled on law and local government. The colonists created a council of five to consult with the governor, who had a double vote at all the meetings.

Besides the menace of extinction through starvation, disease, or the savages, and the risks from bad characters sent from Europe, there was constant danger from the Puritan party, the bishops, and the king, lest they should be robbed of their religious freedom, and their democracy be destroyed. Such a thing as self-government was hateful to more than one party in the England of that day.

In 1623 Robert Gorges sent out another company of settlers to Weymouth, and among them was an Episcopal clergyman, the Rev. William Morrell, to whom was granted power to regulate and control religious affairs in all the region about. This gave Bradford new trouble, though in a letter which was brought by the ship Charity, he had been warned by Robinson of what was likely to happen. But when Morrell came into the new land of America, he found himself one of the pioneers of that long and interesting list of failures who have tried to make a political church and other old world notions work in the new world, and who discover that what is appropriate, historical, and beautiful in Europe may be ugly, unsuitable, and worthless in the new world. Morrell, however, was a man of character and good sense. He became a student and an observer, but attempted no exercise of any authority. Even the "Particulars" could not make a tool of him.

Somewhat like "Churchmen" of England who became "Dissenters" in Scotland, the Pilgrims, who had themselves been Separatists, were now of the "established" religion, and found a body of nonconformists among themselves. Their wisdom was taxed to the uttermost in dealing with the new problem, for the "Particulars" among them sent back complaining letters to the Merchant Adventurers in London, giving rather a dark picture, as it seemed to them, of the state of religious affairs in the colony.

When the Charity returned in 1624 with cows and provisions, she brought, besides a catechism from the Adventurers requiring answers, Master John Lyford, his wife, and four children. This gentleman, a Puritan preacher in the state church, had been sent in defiance of the protest of Winslow and Cushman, who were at the meeting which voted the mission, and through whom it was settled that Lyford should have no official power, except as the church at Plymouth should grant it. At first Lyford was all obsequiousness; but soon the heads of himself, of Oldham, and of others among the "Particulars" were so frequently together, that Bradford's suspicions were aroused, and he took a bold step, which, in the weak state of the colony, was like that of a cony fighting a hedgehog. He intercepted the letters which had been put on board the ship to be sent to England. After Oldham, the organizer of the elements of disturbance, had quarreled with Standish, refusing to do sentinel duty, calling the captain names, and even drawing a knife, for which he was put into the guard-house, Bradford confronted the plotters in a general town meeting with the intercepted letters. These had recommended that John Robinson be kept out of the colony, that Miles Standish should be deposed, and another captain appointed, while very serious charges were made against the colony in general. The court voted that the ringleaders should be expelled from the settlement, but that Lyford might remain six months longer. The parson, thus put on probation, lived at Plymouth during the winter of 1624. He then joined Oldham at Nantasket. When, in 1625, Oldham visited Plymouth, only to revile the colonists as rebels and traitors, he was put into jail. After this, he was led out between two lines of armed men, each of whom gave him a mild rap as he moved along, and he was thus ignominiously expelled from the colony. Possibly the Indians taught the whites this military punishment of running the "gauntlet," though it may have been introduced by Standish from the Dutch army.

Bradford justified his action by showing that to receive a man empowered to work mischief by the politico-religious machine, at the head of which was Archbishop Laud and King James, would be like the cony which on a stormy day allowed the hedgehog to share its quarters. This, in the end, meant that the creature with the prickly spines had the whole of the borough to itself.

The Merchant Adventurers in London were very angry with this act of the colony, and when Winslow came over early in 1625, the company charged the colony with being "Brownists."

They demanded, as the conditions of further co-operation, that the Pilgrims should adopt the French or Presbyterian discipline, both in substance and detail; and that their old pastor and leader, John Robinson, should not be allowed to join them, unless they should first reconcile themselves by written recantation with "our church," — by which they meant, not only the venerable and beautiful Episcopal form of Christianity, but the political machine associated with it, at the head of which were James Stuart and William Laud.

The brave answer of this little company of Christians on a strange continent and between the wilderness and the sea, showed their true temper and knowledge of the Scriptures. It proved also that John Robinson's teaching had not been forgotten. It served to authenticate his parting words. The Pilgrims declared that their discipline was in harmony with that of the Reformed churches. They instanced the example of Paul, who would have no man follow him except as he followed Christ. Neither would they allow that any man or any church corporation had "so sounded the Word of God in all its depths, as to be able to set down precisely the church or discipline without error in substance or circumstance."

By their bold answer the Pilgrims won and held their freedom. The faction among the Adventurers who were hostile to freedom of conscience, even in America, dropped out of view. The other party favorable to the Plymouth men wrote encouragingly, and, stating that fourteen hundred pounds were due, asked that the debt should be met as soon as agreeable. The Plymouth leaders joyfully hailed this as their opportunity. In the summer of 1625 Miles Standish went across the ocean to buy out the Adventurers, so that the colonists could be free in possession of their goods and lands as well as in their conscience. Though times were hard, money very difficult to borrow, and the plague was raging in London, Standish had some success. He returned after five months, bringing news and letters from their two former homes. King James, Maurice the stadholder, and John Robinson were dead.

Despite the partial failure of Standish's mission, the prospects of the colonists improved from this time forth. Evidently more care and pains were taken in the conduct of trade. Material for traffic with the Indians fortunately came to their hands, when the English trading-post at Monhegan was about to break up. Bradford and Winslow went thither in an open boat. With David Thompson, of Piscataqua, they joined forces, and bought the whole stock for about eight hundred pounds. This they divided equally, getting some goats among the property. From their first arrival they had dogs, swine, and poultry, but no cattle until the Charity came, in 1624, with a bull and three heifers. A French ship loaded with rugs and other material was wrecked at Sagadahoc. This equipped them finely with more material. The next question was how to build a larger boat, that they might extend their trade. They cut the shallop in half, added six feet in the middle, and put on a deck.

With their renovated craft, they were able to go up the Kennebec River so far as where Augusta, the capital of Maine, now stands, and there work up a fine trade. They also sent Allerton, who was the most skillful trader among them, to London to conclude the bargain begun by Standish. Allerton was able to borrow two hundred pounds at thirty per cent., and this he invested carefully in goods for the comfort of the plantation. He had also contracted with the Adventurers, buying off their entire interest at eighteen hundred pounds, to be paid in installments of two hundred pounds yearly, in London. The responsibility for this radical stroke of business was assumed by the "firm" of "undertakers," Bradford, Standish, Allerton, Winslow, Howland, Alden, and Prence, who, thus, by being bondsmen, became virtually the owners of the plantation. Allerton returned on a fishing-vessel to Maine, and thence got to Plymouth.

Having taken so great a responsibility in one line of policy by making themselves vouchers for the colony, the "firm" became "undertakers" in another direction, — toward the colonists themselves. They agreed to import every year fifty pounds' worth of shoes and stockings, monopolizing also the trade outside the colony, and using as they pleased the boats, equipments, and trading material. On the other hand, the colonists were to buy of the "undertakers" their hosiery and footgear, paying therefor three bushels of corn or six pounds of tobacco, and at the end of the six years the whole of the trade was to return to the use and benefit of the colony as before. The purchasers numbered about one hundred and fifty-six in all, of whom ninety-one were males, or fifty-seven men and thirty-four boys, and sixty-five females, of whom twenty-nine were matrons and thirty-six were girls. There were also twenty or thirty servants or apprentices.

The eight men, who were "undertakers," or securities, now reorganized the little community, dividing the land into shares of twenty acres each, giving to each settler, described and enrolled as a purchaser, one share in addition to the land he already possessed. The heads of households were, of course, each to have as many shares as there were persons in their families. This new plan put the "Particulars" on the same level with the "Generals." The meadow-land, however, was held as common.

In other words, here was the village community system, in which the rights of the individual were recognized along with the common ownership of land. This had been the original mode of life in Friesland and in New Netherland, as well as in Anglo-Saxon England and at Plymouth. It seems to be a natural order.

No cattle, as has been said, were in the settlement until 1624, though there were dogs, swine, and poultry. In 1625 there were nine and in 1627 twelve cows. These were then so apportioned that there was one cow to thirteen persons, the cattle, like the land, being assigned by lot to each of the divisions. The cows were probably of both English and Dutch stock. One was blind, another was noted for smooth horns, and one or two were red. The more numerous references to black and white, however, show that most of the herd were of the Holstein-Friesland breed so famous and frequent in Holland. The descriptions of their colors and horns show that they were well known by sight but not by names, for the Pilgrims were such stalwart realists that they had apparently little sentiment in the giving of names, except to their children.

This year, 1627, begins the Pilgrims' book of Numbers. After their Genesis, or beginning, in England, their Exodus, or going out to Holland, their Leviticus in Leyden, where their polity and worship were shaped, came the fourth phase of their development. Henceforth we have in their books of records the story of their methodical arrangements, lists of names, inventories, statistics, and treasury accounts, which remind us of the fourth book of the Pentateuch, and recall the older Pilgrim's Progress, which was led by Moses and written by him or his successors. Counting those who had come to stay, or had been born in New Plymouth, the total number was two hundred and sixty-seven. Fifty-eight had died, and fifty-three had removed. After the first awful winter, the colonists were so healthy that but six persons died during the succeeding six years.

From this year, 1627, their finances were established on a sound basis. As once they had found shelter from persecution and many years of life and comfort in Holland, so now from the Dutch in America they were to learn the secret of wealth by getting from them the idea and the reality of Indian currency. Their old neighbor in Leyden, Jesse de Forest, had at last persuaded both his Walloon friends and the Dutch government to start permanent colonies of men, women, and children on Manhattan Island and in the Hudson and Mohawk river valleys. By 1627 there were two hundred and seventy people in New Netherland, who had over one hundred cattle. Although the Dutch claimed the territory in which the Pilgrims had settled, they had too much to attend to at home to urge their claims; but in March, 1627, Bradford was pleasantly surprised on receiving a friendly letter from the secretary of the West India Company's government at Manhattan. With true republican courtesy, that recognized untitled citizens as "noble, worshipful, the wise and prudent lords," — especially if they were really so, — the Dutch authorities addressed the governor and counselors residing in "Nieu-Pliemuen" (or New Plymouth), and, after wishing them temporal and eternal happiness, expressed a desire for kindly intercourse. Now that the mother countries beyond sea had renewed their league, they would meet their English friends for trade wherever desired.

The secretary, Isaac de Rasieres, was evidently one, or the son of one, of those Walloons, or Belgian French, of the Reformed faith, who had, like the Pilgrims, come to Holland for religious freedom. It shows how well Dutch was understood among these late and long residents in Leyden, that the reply to the director and Council of New Netherland, "our very loving friends and Christian neighbors," was in Dutch. It has in it none of that abominable prejudice which disgraces English speech and people, and which Americans have inherited from the old-world naval wars of later times, while it reveals the gratitude, the honesty, and the noble character of the Pilgrims. The Pilgrims were English to the core, yet they were not ashamed, but very glad, to recognize their obligations. Reciprocating the Dutch friendship, this occasion was taken for expressing grateful remembrance of the way the Pilgrims had been treated in Holland.

One passage from a letter is as follows: "Acknowledging ourselves tied in a strict obligation into your country and state, for the good entertainment and free liberty we had, and our brethren and countrymen yet there have, and do enjoy under your most honorable Lords and States . . . for which we are bound to be thankful and our children after us."

With a characteristic English thriftiness and love of honorable gain, and with an eye to the main chance quite equal to the Dutch, and wishing, withal, to keep out of difficulties, Bradford cautioned his neighbors against settling within the territory claimed by England. He requested them not to trade in the field already occupied by the Plymouth men, around Buzzard's Bay or the Narragansett and Sowams region.

Meanwhile in Leyden, on March 4, 1625, John Robinson had died. There are two Dutch records of the burial. The city census of October, 1622, enrolled him and his wife Bridget; his children, John, Bridget, Isaac, Mercy, Fear, and James; and their servant maid, Mary Hardy. Isaac Robinson, the ancestor of a host of good people, came to America in 1631. The congregation in Leyden flourished until 1658, when, being more Dutch than English, it united with the Reformed Church.

CHAPTER XIX

A VISIT FROM MANHATTAN

In the following August, 1627, the government at Manhattan sent a firm and respectful answer to Plymouth Colony, intimating that the territory between the fortieth and forty-fifth parallels of north latitude was claimed by the Dutch Congress, or States-General, as well as by the English king; that its right to trade was as good as that of the Pilgrims, and that this claim would be maintained. The bearer of this letter was John Jacobson, who was from Wieringen, an island in the Zuyder Zee near the Helder. This Hollander was pleasantly entertained at Plymouth, and took back a letter from Bradford, kind, but firm, asserting that any intruders on their domain of trade would be expelled by force. He requested that a Dutch officer from Manhattan should visit them and make a mutual agreement, but gave warning of the danger incurred because of the unscrupulous pirates and kidnappers infesting the coast. Should they fall into the hands of the privateersmen, or those of Virginia, or the fishing-ships which came to Maine from England, they would suffer.

The Dutch responded promptly and sent their secretary, Isaac de Rasieres, who on the 4th of October, in the bark Nassau, came to Buzzard's Bay, at Manomet, or Sandwich, where the Plymouth men had a trading-house. John Jacobson, being a good pedestrian, tramped in six hours the twenty miles from Manomet to Plymouth, but de Rasieres, being a corpulent gentleman, was not able to walk so far. He feared that his feet would fail him, and asked that a boat be sent. His request was granted, and this first foreign embassy, consisting of the secretary from New Amsterdam, with his trumpeters and some other attendants, came by water. De Rasieres had cloth of three sorts and colors, a chest of white sugar, and some small wares, for which the Plymouth people paid him in home-grown tobacco. Thus began a trade which for many years was one of mutual benefit. It lasted until the Virginians, coming up by sea, diverted it.

Most important of all the results of this meeting of the American Dutch and the American English was that Plymouth learned the use of wampum. The Iroquois, or the confederated Five Nations in New Netherland, were far higher in the scale of civilization than any other Indians north of Mexico. They were traders, as well as fighters, having even a fixed currency. On coming to America the Dutch, with their keen commercial sense, perceived at once the tremendous importance of this shell money for both traffic and diplomacy. They saw that seawant, or wampum, was more than coinage to the men of the forest. Beside being used like pieces and sums of money which circulated among many tribes, even far in the interior, they noted that when strung and wrought into patterns, it was in America what letters, sealed documents, precious vouchers and memorials, and even crown jewels were in Europe. To this day, the ancient traditions and the history of those tribes which still keep their organization are expressed in belts of wampum. Long Island had been named Seawanaka, the island of shells, from its abundance of seawant, or wampum material.

With their superior tools, drills, hammers, knives, and lathes, the men from the land of banks and of the diamond-polishing industry were able quickly to get and to keep the manufacture of wampum almost entirely in their own hands. Some of the Dutch settlements, notably Schenectady, became veritable mints for the making of this kind of money. Here the intelligent and nimble squaws were employed in considerable numbers to string and arrange the perforated beads, which were drilled, ground, and polished by the white men. The wampum made by the Dutch, or by squaws under Dutch oversight, was not only far better, but much more beautiful, than that from the red men's fingers alone. To-day some of the noblest and most striking documents and autographs in American history are of wampum, the archives of the Iroquois being especially interesting. Among other shell muniments is the treaty document of Penn, "never sworn to and never broken."

It was de Rasieres who acquainted Bradford with this money. He thus gave the Pilgrims their first idea of aboriginal currency, and sold them fifty pounds' worth. Among the Algonquin Indians wampum was then not much known, if at all, east of Narragansett Bay. At first the Pilgrims may have thought that the Dutch had overreached them, for it was nearly two years before their red neighbors took up even the fifty pounds' worth of shell money; but after that time, the eastern Indians having learned its benefits, the Plymouth men could hardly supply it fast enough. Meanwhile these Indians had learned how to drill and string similar tokens, which they made from the quahog or big clam shells. Six white beads or three purple ones made from the eye of the clam were worth a penny, or a dime in the values of to-day. The Englishmen were not at first so skillful as the Dutch in making the Indian money, and they could not produce it so cheaply as the Indians made it. Not only was trade stimulated through this business and the Pilgrims enriched, but the Indians also were made wealthier, and now began to buy firearms, which not only the Dutch and French and English fishermen, but probably all of the whites in New England who came to the coast, except the Plymouth men, sold them. In time the red men with their new weapons took courage to begin "King Philip's war."

No extant description of the town of Plymouth, even from the pen of Bradford or Winslow, is so complete and interesting as that of de Rasieres, whose letter to his friend Herr Blommaert, a director of the Dutch West India Company, is in the Royal Library at the Hague. He pictures the town and the ceremonious way of attending divine worship on Sunday. When the drum beat, the men assembled in front of Captain Standish's door, each with his musket or firelock, and in cold weather having on their cloaks. Forming ranks three abreast, the sergeant led them without beat of the drum to the church. Behind the guard walked the governor, who had on his right hand the preacher, and on the left hand the captain, who carried a little stick in his hand. They marched in good order, and in the meeting-house each one set his gun near him. Thus they were vigilant day and night. "Their government is after the English form," the election being held annually; but in inheritance the Pilgrims had discarded English primogeniture and followed the Dutch method of placing the children all in one degree, making only a nominal acknowledgment to the oldest son, on account of the seniority of birth. De Rasieres praised warmly the high morality of the Pilgrims, showing how they influenced also the Indians to nobler living. He even criticises severely the Dutch in the Hudson River region.

In appraising the exact value of de Rasieres's letter we must not lose sight of the subjective element, or of local politics and of commercial or ecclesiastical jealousies, with which the Dutch, like the English, were afflicted. De Rasieres, who wrote when his fellow-countrymen in New Netherland were without a church or a minister, and in the year before the Rev. J. Michaelius came to organize a church in New Amsterdam, had already lost his position through some faction. Then, his one great idea was to show in the darkest colors possible how bad was the government at Manhattan, how low the morals of those who had displaced him, and how wicked the people were. As a matter of course, he takes without criticism what his friends at New Plymouth tell him, and uses the information in order to rub brine into the wounds of those whom he would injure.

Financial freedom for Plymouth Colony was gradually and slowly won as wampum was more and more used, and as the beaver skins sent over to England brought good prices.

Although the Plymouth men never possessed a royal charter, yet in 1629 the Council of New

England, the Earl of Warwick being president, granted to the colony a new patent, dated January 23, 1630, which for the first time defined the limits of territory, including a grant of land for fifteen miles on each side of the Kennebec River. This charter, with the compact framed at Cape Cod in 1620, formed the basis of government. The colony was to follow the laws of England "as near as may be."

The Plymouth men having built a fortified trading-house on the present site of Augusta, Maine, and stocked it with dry goods and clothing, rugs and blankets, corn and biscuit and dried fruit, knives, hatchets, and wampum, were getting much beaver in return and making money. Their financial prosperity, however, came near having a dangerous setback because the over-adventurous Allerton exceeded his authority, mismanaging the funds and getting the colonists in debt to the amount of nearly five thousand pounds, while they were owing one thousand pounds. Nevertheless, their excellent trade, good crops and fisheries, and the application of experience to business enabled them to pay off all their debts in 1633, so that at the end of that year they owed no man anything but love.

The red Indians were not the only immediate enemies who threatened to break up the settlement at Plymouth. There were dangerous characters among the miscellaneous white men that now began to get a foothold along the seashore. One of these was the infamous Thomas Morton, of Merrymount. This renegade lawyer from London, after inciting a rebellion among the indentured servants at Quincy, in the absence of his partner, or employer, Wollaston, opened a lively trade with the red men, and with his companions spent his spare time in drunkenness and worse wickedness. They brought in Indian squaws, laid in a supply of rum, and erected a Maypole decorated with rhymes of Morton's own writing. Then the squaws and whites joined in the revels with dances, Morton being the chief. The whites sold arms to the Indians, employing them to hunt for them and get furs.

Still further and worse, these communists welcomed to their company whatever white men would join them. This made the situation dangerous, not only to Plymouth, but to the other colonies, some ten in number, that were scattered about in Massachusetts and New Hampshire. With stalwart hunters suddenly changed from the stone age, so far as opportunity to do mischief was concerned, and becoming expert marksmen with firearms, and Merrymount liable to be an Adullam's cave, where unruly servants and lawless characters could find refuge, there were dangers worse than those of an Indian plot. For the safety of all the colonists, King James had, in 1622, forbidden the sale of guns to the Indians.

Respectful letters were sent to Morton calling his attention to this fact, and urging him to be loyal and obedient. His reply was one of defiance.

Thereupon Governor Bradford was implored to enforce the laws by military aid. Standish liked nothing better than to attempt the enterprise. Probably, since Morton had called the short and fiery captain "Captain Shrimp," he had the spur to his pride to show what a shrimp could do. When Morton saw the Plymouth armed men approaching, he got ready his ammunition and loaded his own gun until it was nearly half full. After setting out plenty of powder and bullets where they would be handy, he began to suspect that his barricades would not help him and might be set on fire. So he gallantly led out his followers, who, unfortunately, were full of liquor. He advanced on Standish, but the little captain pushed Morton's gun to one side and seized the commander of Merrymount. The only blood shed was from the nose of a drunken man of the garrison, who lost a little of his hot ichor by running against a sword. The historian of the Netherlands, John Lothrop Motley, who made these episodes the basis of his novel "Merrymount," writes of the victor, "Miles in name, leagues in valor, and but a few paltry inches in stature."

Morton was taken prisoner to Plymouth, and then sent to England in charge of an agent; but when in the old country Sir Ferdinando Gorges, being a favorite at court, had the good "churchman" saved from punishment, as having been persecuted by the "Brownists." Shielded by Laud, Morton twice visited Plymouth, and was expelled. In 1637 he published a scurrilous book full of lies and slander, under the title "The New English Canaan." Turning up again in Plymouth in 1643, Morton lived there during the winter, sometimes shooting birds over Captain Standish's land, evidently with the idea of getting into a quarrel, and thus bringing the Plymouth men into trouble with the government of London. Being unsuccessful, he went to Boston and then to Piscataqua, where he sank out of sight and died.

By this time Plymouth plantation had spread beyond its original bounds, for the people were learning the country. They began to see that the soil was much better in the interior. They had settled on the old glacier drift, but the river valleys and the bottom-lands were much richer. Going farther inland they fared better. Hence we find many graves, of both the old comers and the newer arrivals, but especially of those of the second and the third generations of the Pilgrims, in central Massachusetts or in States adjacent. Furthermore, as the cattle increased, their owners were compelled to go farther afield for a pasture. At first they built summer huts and encampments wherein to stay between frosts; but later they erected winter dwellings. Thus gradually various villages were formed.

Miles Standish, William Brewster, and John Alden went to live in Duxbury, around which are places with old names, showing that Londoners settled the second town of the Old Colony. Edward Winslow obtained land at Green Harbor, afterwards known as Marshfield. This was the third of the eight separate towns which existed when, in 1643, following the example of the federal Dutch republic, the New England confederation proposed by the Plymouth men was formed. These towns were Plymouth, Duxbury, Marshfield, Scituate, Barnstable, Taunton, Yarmouth, and Sandwich.

By this time, also, despite all their difficulties, opposition at home and abroad, and the determination of the faction among the Adventurers to keep further "Brownists" from coming to them from Leyden, the men and women of New Plymouth — for the women, no less than the men, were factors in the case — had demonstrated the success of their plantation.

Animated by the shining example of success of the Pilgrim company, there now began from England, thanks to the tyranny of Charles Stuart and the persecution of Laud, a great movement of emigration, lasting from 1628 to 1640, during which no fewer than twenty-three thousand

English, Scottish, Welsh, and Irish people came to America; or more than the whole number from 1640 to 1775. The English immigrants, though representing forty counties, were chiefly from that eastern side of England, which, having always been so close to the Continent, was quick to respond to reformatory and civilizing movements, and which was not only nearest to the Netherlands, but was richer in Netherlandish blood, having been for a thousand years continually reënforced by fresh emigrations of Saxons, Angles, Frisians, and Dutchmen. God makes the best manhood out of a composite of the best human stocks.

CHAPTER XX

LAW AND PUNISHMENT

THE Pilgrim republic was a true prototype of the United States of America, cosmopolitan, tolerant, Christian. Here were people of at least seven nationalities, of varying degrees of character, culture, and social standing, and of different creeds and ideas of government in church and state. Yet into this colony men of all sects and of no sect were received if they were willing to obey the laws and usages. With an intense and positive faith, the Pilgrims made no form of words to bind the conscience. They welcomed to their church fellowship all who made Jesus Christ their teacher and model. To safeguard their own organism, they warned off and kept off all who proposed to destroy their freedom or to introduce anarchy or revolution.

Yet even among themselves there were characters "shuffled in," as Bradford says, who were dangerous to the peace and integrity of the settlement. Stocks had been used in most European and perhaps all English towns and villages prior to this time, but were not put up in Plymouth until necessity compelled their erection. There would have been use for them so early as 1621, or before the Pilgrims had been on shore more than five months. Billington, whose sons had already given him and others so much trouble, on refusing to obey some order of Captain Standish, was tied neck and heels together and put in a public place before the whole settlement. Two servants who wanted to fight a duel were served in like manner.

In 1630 Billington, being angry with John Newcomen, for interfering in some way with his hunting, waylaid and fired at him, mortally wounding him. The murderer was arrested, and by regular process of trial by jury condemned to be hanged. He pleaded for his life, questioning also the authority of the colony to inflict capital punishment, and the matter was referred to the Puritan Governor Winthrop and his counselors as a court of appeals. Their answer was that Billington ought to die and the land be purged from blood. Greatly to the grief of the Plymouth men, who made their feelings give way to conscience, they carried out the sentence.

Goodwin, in his "Pilgrim Republic," notes the fact that in Plymouth town of to-day "the public places so rarely bear the names interwoven with her early history, and that the few exceptions commemorate Allerton the treacherous, Shirley the defrauder, and Billington the malefactor." As a matter of fact, there is very little that shows much sentiment, in the ordinary meaning of the term, among the Pilgrim company; certainly very little, such as later artists and poets have suggested in the transfiguring creations of their imagination. One does not find, except in the names of towns, much to suggest either their old Fatherland or their home during their stay in Holland. Those names which, like Leyden Street, seem to recall memories or to breathe gratitude are of modern suggestion and by their descendants. There is not yet any town in the United States named Scrooby, Austerfield, or Bawtry. Not only were the Pilgrim Separatists not much given to surface sentiment, and certainly never to weak sentimentalism, but we must remember that for one whole generation after reaching America, they were looked upon by their Puritan neighbors as "Brownists," and were spoken of with contempt. Even in the second and third generation this offensive epithet was more or less in use.

Probably the real reason for the absence of place names redolent of sentiment or gratitude was a political one. The special use of English or Dutch names of their old homes would have looked like defiance or disloyalty to King James. Little as we realize it now, the hostility of the throne and church in England, until Cromwell's time, was a constant menace of death to the Pilgrim church and republic.

In these phenomena of history and phases of human nature there is nothing extraordinary. Whether it be a great man or a great idea, it takes humanity a long time to appreciate what is excellent. Whether it be Jesus of Nazareth, or Paul, or St. Francis of Assisi, or Oliver Cromwell, or Abraham Lincoln, or the Pilgrims, or the Methodists, or the Anabaptists, or the Mikado-reverencers, time is necessary for the truth to rise clear of the murky vapors and impure media through which men look. Only after ages can some truths be seen shining as clear as the sun by day and as bright as the stars by night. Yet "time at last sets all things even," and truth is safe, for "the eternal years of God are hers." To-day all that the Pilgrims need is to have their story told without embroidery, without detraction. The narrative itself is an epic.

The legislation and punishments of the Old Colony period are to-day subjects for amusement as well as for reflection. These Englishmen at Plymouth were of the seventeenth and not of the nineteenth century. The old comers brought with them the legal ideas and the social customs which they had seen in vogue in England and Holland. Vice and crime were dealt with no worse, and usually better than had been the case in the England which they had seen. The second generation, as has been so often illustrated in other colonies, was of ruder manners and of a lower grade of intelligence than had been the first immigrants. Those who had not been educated in England and mellowed in Holland, or had never joined in the mirth and sports of either of the older countries, were harsher and less intelligent, as well as more narrow and superstitious. Indeed, this seems to be the rule among people not born in the old seats of civilization, who must yet be pioneers in subduing the wilderness. Social improvement usually comes with later generations. There is little doubt, also, that by being confederate with the Puritans, from 1643 to 1686, the Plymouth men lost in manliness and in self-reliance what they gained in political security and mercantile success. So also in the making of their laws and in the cast of their minds, the second generation was less reasonable than the first. The theological climate was much more rigorous, and the intolerance of youth and the reversion to mere animal instincts were more noticeable.

The stocks were often put to use. This means of punishment is especially an English institution, going back to the Middle Ages. It was sometimes found even at the church porch, for correcting a variety of offenders. Beside their own home-grown malefactors, the Plymouth men sometimes kept their stocks well warmed by Friends to whom they were not friends. The stocks were a great aid to good order in the meeting-house, for any one caught laughing, joking, flirting or asleep, especially if such practices were persisted in, was dragged out by the tithingman and framed to make a public picture. These oaken timbers had openings for the legs and arms. While sitting on the bench or stool, with legs held helpless in the notches of the beams, every small boy and idle person could jeer at the poor victim.

We can imagine many a scene in Plymouth where with horn lantern and staff in hand the magistrate at night went after some victim whom he dragged out of bed, to put in timber locks. Then the next day, boys and girls, straggling Indians, and surprised fathers and mothers would go out to see the man or woman held helplessly in shameful plight. Sometimes a written paper, describing the crime of the person disgraced, was nailed up.

The stocks, ducking-stools, pillory, whipping-post and gag were temporary punishments borrowed from England, but the continuous wearing of a shameful badge for any offense was probably not of English, but of continental origin. We all know what a romantic story Nathaniel Hawthorne has made of "The Scarlet Letter." This badge of shame was not imaginary, but real. In mediæval Europe it was not only the custom to compel the criminal to wear letters indicative of crime, such as *I* for incest, *A* for adultery, and *T* for thief, but even the Jews were compelled to wear a certain article of dress or a mark to declare their generation. Lepers, other diseased persons, and heretics were also branded. These social scars were made first with the hot iron upon the skin, just as slaves were branded with owners' names. Later, as the laws were ameliorated, the embroidered or painted letter was made a substitute for the brand in the flesh.

The following is one of several similar entries in the records of the Plymouth Colony:[1] "At this court, Catheren Kaines . . . is sentenced by the court to be forthwith publicly whipped here at Plymouth and afterwards at Taunton on a public training day and to wear a Roman B cut out of red cloth and sewed to her open garment on her right arm; and if she shall be ever found without it so worn while she is in the government to be forthwith publicly whipped." This was for blasphemy. Among letters employed in Plymouth justice were *B* for blasphemy, *D* for drunkenness, *V* for viciousness, and so on.

We never hear of, nor could we imagine books being condemned to the fire in Plymouth, as was the case in Boston in 1650, with Mr. William Pynchon's work on "A Meritorious Price of Our Redemption." Indeed, this was not the only time that books were burned or authors whipped in Boston, — the city which now has Pynchon's name on one of its streets and is so hospitable to new ideas.

[1] Vol. iii. pp. 111 and 112, 1656–57, 5 March, Bradford Governor.

The Englishmen in America set up the whipping-post very quickly after their arrival. They were not particular whether the skins welted with the scourge were white, black, or red. The work of stripe-making was often done on lecture days and even on Sundays. This punishment was inflicted for profanity, perjury, lying, selling firewater to the Indians, or for even sleeping in church. Neither women nor men were spared. In 1638 the court in Plymouth found that " divers persons unfit for marriage, both in regard of their young years as also in regard of their weak estate, some practicing the inveigling of men's daughters and maids and contrary to their parents' and guardians' liking, and of maid servants without the leave and liking of their masters," ordered punishment either by fine or flogging. No doubt the behavior of the victims or the officers of law furnished a good deal of amusement, revealing also a lack of sensitiveness to human suffering, — just as in old Japan the public decapitation of criminals always brought, and in the China to-day brings, a crowd of spectators from Christian nations. In Plymouth there must have been a good deal of public whipping, both of women and men, when suffering mingled with the noise of the mob; but even this judicial flagellation was insignificant, compared with what was done in some other colonies.

After all that can be truthfully said of Puritan rigor or Pilgrim severity, the punishments were worse in the southern colonies than in the northern, but far below the standard of justice tempered with mercy which prevailed in the middle colonies. That portion of the New Europe in America settled under the more enlightened ideas of the Netherlanders avoided the extremes of both Cavalier and Puritan. Being under the sway of milder and more Christian legislation and custom, the empire region of the middle colonies was more free from unreasonably cruel punishments.

The legislation of the Plymouth Colony, while closely conformable to that of the rest of the world in Christendom, was singularly free from the extremes seen in the rest of New England and in the southern colonies. It was wonderfully like that of the Netherlands, where both in government and custom Christianity and civilization were then much better illustrated. On the statute books of Plymouth there were fewer capital crimes named than in any other colonies north or south of New York and Pennsylvania. The Plymouth law decreeing the death sentence upon Quakers was passed late in their history and was never enforced. The spirit of the Pilgrims had been chastened by their persecutions, sufferings, and exile and by dwelling in a tolerant republic, which was then the leader among nations.

CHAPTER XXI

FOOD, DRESS, AND SOCIAL LIFE

LET us see how the Plymouth people ate their food, and what kind of a diet the men would be able to provide and the women to cook, dress, and serve. Within ten or twenty years after that first awful winter, life had settled down to steady routine. Living in timber houses, at first very rough, mud-plastered, with thatched roof and greased paper windows, neither furniture nor household adornment could have been anything but the simplest. As time sped on and they became better acquainted with the resources of the country, and the ships from Europe brought over more numerous comforts, the homes became brighter and cheerier, and approached more nearly the standard of daily life in Europe.

The era of hot drinks imported from the far East, and first used in Holland, had not yet come. During the first years of the colony, tea, coffee, and Delft or Japan ware were things probably merely heard of, and even in the later years were curiosities. Not until toward the end, in 1691, did they become even luxuries to be enjoyed by a few.

Beer was the every-day drink among the Plymouth people. Those who could not afford this drank water. Rarely was a piece of china seen upon the table, though earthenware was occasionally in use. Most of the dishes, apart from the mugs and cups, were of wood or of pewter. All well-to-do housekeepers took pride in polishing their metal ware, making it shine like silver, and adorning their mantelpieces, shelves, and cupboards with the platters and dishes.

Tobacco, the seed of which the Pilgrims obtained from the red men, was grown at Plymouth and formed in the first years, until the better Virginia article displaced it, a small crop. The men often refreshed themselves with its fumes, but usually did so indoors. In 1638 a law forbade smoking in the streets. The legislation against drunkenness in one's house, the sale of spiritous liquors to Indians, or in quantities to cause intoxication, was stringent. The idea was prohibition to Indians and temperance among the whites.

In our minds' pictures, we may imagine the people sitting down to their tables made of hewn wood, smoothed by the axe, and on stools or benches made of the same material and in the same fashion. Only the well-to-do folk had rush-bottomed chairs from the old land. Governor Carver's chair is preserved to this day, and is an exact copy of those still found in rural Holland.

The Mayflower of legend — the ship which had no more real existence than the Flying Dutchman — sailed into Plymouth Harbor apparently with her decks loaded and all her spars hung with old furniture, teapots, luxurious table-ware, and miscellaneous household stuff. The historic ship had room for very little indeed except the passengers and their personal apparel and equipment.

In the American colonies, as elsewhere in Christendom, the Oriental hot drinks proved a powerful factor, not only in developing the ceramic art, but in the social elevation of women. The mother took her place at the head of the table. Teapot, sugar-bowl, and cream-pitcher, or jug, became of more importance than the salt-cellar or spice-box.

Knives were plentiful, but spoons less so, while forks were unknown. Large or long-handled prongs were used to turn the meat in the pot, but a table fork for each person was probably never seen in Plymouth Colony. The meat was held with the fingers and cut in pieces on the platter, and the bits taken to the mouth by the unassisted hand. Forks became fashionable first in Italy, and the nine hundredth anniversary of their introduction was celebrated in 1897. Among English people, until late in the seventeenth century, they were curiosities as great as umbrellas would have been at that time even in London. The prehistoric men used a certain kind of fork, just as the Fiji Islanders did until their conversion to Christianity during this century, but most probably only at their cannibal feasts.

Well-to-do people, in the days when vegetables were very few and when all kinds of spices were in demand, sprinkled saffron upon their meat; and in Essex, from which county many settlers of Massachusetts came, this plant was so much cultivated that one place was called Saffron Walden. Its powder made an agreeable flavor, was easily dissolved in water, and was not injurious. It was quite common, before forks came into use, to see the left-hand fingers of ladies yellow with the stain. The word "saffron" was often used as a verb, even as we see in Chaucer.

As napkins and hand-wipers were quite necessary on the Pilgrims' tables, so we find them to have been very common.

Vegetables were comparatively few. The white potato was unknown, and the sweet potato was not common until the next century. The food for the children would be milk and corn-meal pudding, or, to use a mongrel word, "porridge." Although other grains were cultivated and white bread was at first most popular, and rye bread well known, yet Indian corn was always the great staple for the making of what Defoe calls "the staff of life." Beside the various kinds of puddings and bake-stuff made from the cereal grains, pease and beans were much employed for soups and stews. Other vegetables cultivated and used were pumpkins, beans, squashes, turnips, parsnips, and onions. In the course of time, in the Dutch ovens, which the Pilgrim women knew so well how to use, began the evolution of those substantial and nutritious dishes, baked beans, brown bread, codfish balls, and pumpkin pies. Other delicacies, such as strawberry shortcake, for which New England has a well-deserved reputation, either as every-day affairs, as Sunday morning features, or as dishes in season, took their places upon the tables.

Fresh fish was always common, but unsalted beef, mutton, and lamb were not. After the excellent stock of the imported Dutch and English cattle had multiplied, the products of the cow were abundant and much enjoyed. Butter and cheese were staple articles. With maize so plenty, the old word "corn" — which was Dutch before it was English — came to mean *the* corn, that is, maize. Since fish, both salt and fresh, was every-day food, the term "meat" was gradually restricted to what is raised on land and furnished by the butcher, and not drawn from the sea and provided by the fisherman, so that the phrase "butcher's meat" fell out of vogue. Instead of being used as the opposite of drink, the word referred to flesh food only.

Gradually there grew up a necessary and proper difference in some phases of English as spoken on this side of the Atlantic. As fashions changed and thought widened on both sides of the ocean, language grew, and there were deaths and survivals of words not known except to scholars and critical readers of Shakespeare. What are called "Americanisms" by the ill-informed are often living descendants of very old-fashioned English speech. Not a few such expressions still used in the Eastern States are classic English, and may be found, not only in the poets and prose writers before the age of the Stuarts, but even yet in rural England.

We are certain about one thing, and that is that these God-fearing and God-loving people always looked first to the Giver of their refreshment and sustenance, never eating until they had bowed their head to "say grace" or rising from the table until they had returned thanks. These joyful Pilgrims were not drunk with wine, wherein is excess, but they were filled with the spirit. They reveled in the life of the soul as well as in that of the body. To a Plymouth dinner of boiled clams and a cup of cold water, they brought as grateful hearts as when before an English feast or a Leyden banquet. Good digestion waited on appetite, health on both, and genuinely filial religion over all.

How did they dress? It is not very difficult to answer this question, for the abundant oil paintings, etchings, copper and wood cuts of Holland and the prints and literature of England, with their own records and relics, make the matter tolerably plain. Muslin or cotton goods were very rare until the days of the Plymouth Colony were nearly over, but wool, hemp, and flax were staple materials.

Linen being very cheap in Holland during the seventeenth century, we are not surprised that men, maids, and matrons were well provided with stores of napery, which they used with æsthetic effect upon their tables as well as in their outward clothing. Stiffened with starch, the snowy fabric helped conspicuously to make a costume that was beautiful and serviceable. The true Puritan, whether in France or Holland or England, dressed neatly and becomingly in a style that would have delighted an ancient Greek, even as it charms many a modern artist.

In the first generation of their history in the old home-land, the Puritans wore woolen coats, and breeches which ended at the knee and were tied together with strings having ornamented tags, their lower limbs being encased in stockings or hose. In the second generation starch and linen became more common. The old ruff had disappeared, and in its place was the rolling or falling collar, usually tied with a white string and tassels.

The dress of the women was simple but unquestionably artistic. We may be quite sure that, Pilgrims though they were, the Plymouth maids were particular about getting the proper fit of shoe, and wearing their stockings without ridges or loose wrinkles. Their skirts were sensibly short, and they were warmly dressed in woolen material, their bodices being either made plainly or laced together over some white or bright colored underdress, while at their shoulders and sleeves they were fond of slashing or opening the woolen fabric so as to show the white underdress. Upon their heads they wore linen caps of snow-like hue, or often simply a top piece with lace, and they had lace at the end of their cuffs toward the shoulders. Over their bosoms and shoulders they usually wore, in time of rest or on special occasions, a white handkerchief, or often one large handkerchief underneath, with a smaller one like a collar over it, displaying their throat and a little of the upper chest. In the season of frost and ice, they had often a bow and necktie also. Sometimes this upper white dress had a lace fringe at the bottom, going around the shoulders and higher part of the bust. Doubtless the long gauntleted gloves were not absent. In winter time, at least, the bonnets or close fitting caps of velvet did not lack either bows at the top or strings gracefully tied under the chin.

No perverted theories of Puritanism, however rigid, could kill or conceal the innate love of beauty which God has implanted in woman's nature. While kings and queens, gallants and ladies might think themselves properly arrayed in costumes which more properly befitted the theatre, the Puritans, not "in spite of themselves," but guided by the unerring law of Greek art and of eternal beauty, which lays more stress on form than on decoration, created a becoming and beautiful type of dress. Having the sheep of the meadow, the flax of the garden, and his own inventive ability, man, male and female, can dress beautifully without the silkworm or the cotton plant.

The spinning-wheel, the direct evolution of the ancient distaff and spindle in union, said to have been invented at Nuremberg so late as 1530, came into Holland first, and then into England, and displaced the old whorl-stones, holding its own until the present century. The deft fingers of the Pilgrim mothers and daughters became very expert in using the spinning-wheel and in making the material for the garments of husbands, children, and kinsfolk. Quite early in the history of the colony, knitting became an industry especially favored by women in their few hours left over from severer toil.

Unlike the Bay Colony, Plymouth never made any law regulating personal costume, and in general kept free of sumptuary legislation. Yet this matter of dress, or rather the necessity of providing the material for it, had become serious in New Plymouth when in 1633 it was forbidden to export any sheep. In 1639 every householder was ordered to sow at least one square rod of flax or hemp. It was only gradually that the distinct trade of webster or weaver became known and recognized in the colony.

Cotton was a great novelty when it made its appearance in New England from the West Indies. This "tree wool" was not woven in England until the eighteenth century, being only rarely seen as a great curiosity. It is no wonder, then, that its nature was not at first well understood. Several children in New England, when first dressed in cotton clothes, were burned to death, and one man whose cotton clothes took fire saved his life by jumping into a well. When, however, the English Civil War broke out, and imports from the home-land were much curtailed, wool became dearer, and cotton was much used for weaving and clothing. By about the year 1666, clothing was so abundant and often made into such attractive forms, that the rather superstitious Morton ascribed the loss of the wheat crop to the wrath of God against the "licentiousness of apparel."

Without doubt both Pilgrim and Puritan, without being foppish or dandyish, set sufficient store upon good clothes. They knew well how great, how continuous was the influence of proper garb upon good manners and even upon character.

Marriage was a frequent episode of life in New Plymouth, for such a thing as an unmarried woman could hardly be known while so many single men wanted mates. There could be no permanent widows or widowers in such primitive life, where the necessity of providing food, and therefore of working hard, was so urgent, for both the most and the best of men's work is done when he has a helpmate with him. Time could not be spared for long mourning or periods of seclusion, and the conventionalities of older and more finished society were out of place.

Very simple indeed were the ceremonies of these first weddings. Both out of principle and from necessity, they were, as Bradford says, after "the laudable custom of the Low Countries." The Pilgrims were Calvinists in their theories. Calvinism, which means realism in religion, did not at first, nor does it now, see any necessity for the minister of religion to be present either at the marriage altar, at the grave, or at the infant's birth, except as an invited servant; though it teaches that God presides over all and that to him each act of man should be consecrated. Believing in the priesthood of all true believers and the equality of all redeemed souls before God, it holds that no child born of Christian parents is unclean. Those Calvinists who admit infants to holy baptism justify it upon the faith of its parents as the true channel of divine grace and fulfillment of the divine promises. Calvinism teaches that marriage is a mystery of love, the fire of God, the union in holy wedlock for the continuance of the race, and the maintenance of purity and obedience to the commands of God. It considers the so-called "consecrated ground" as the invention of sectarian priestcraft and an outrage upon our common humanity.

This being their belief the Pilgrims could not see the need of the "professional mercenary" of the ecclesiastical corporation, even though they might invite and enjoy the presence and services of the modest servant of God and of the church, the minister of the Word. Death, to the believer in Christ who takes the New Testament as his sole guide, is the union of earth to earth, the honorable return of the dissolved earthly house to its original elements, and the rejoining of the spirit to its first home with God. The Pilgrims did not therefore feel that any religious services at the grave-side were necessary, though they felt free to have these if they desired.

In New Plymouth the grand simplicity and divine sufficiency in Christ of men who knew their Bibles well enabled them to marry, to bury, and to bring up their children without the aid of diocesan bishops, church corporations, or priests, or kings. They had, under God, created a state where none of these things were needed. They laid the foundation of a nation in which priest and pastor will ever be servants and not masters of the congregation.

CHAPTER XXII

CUSTOMS AND SUPERSTITIONS

THE Pilgrim wedding ceremony was very simple. The couple were joined in wedlock by the magistrate, though prayer was not omitted. The first marriage took place in the lovely month of May, 1621, when Edward Winslow, whose wife had died but seven weeks before, married Susanna White, a widow with children, whose husband had died twelve weeks before. Mrs. White was the mother of Peregrine, the first child born of white parents in New England. Another son, born after her second marriage, became governor of an American colony, so that this Pilgrim mother has a triple honor. Yet about this historic wedding no poetry has been written, nor of it has any picture been painted or printed. The Pilgrim fathers have had their meed of fame; but the story of the Pilgrim mothers, could it be told aright, would at most points be of equal fascination.

The imagination of poet and artist and popular interest have gathered around another episode of love, courtship, and marriage, all three elements of which were doubtless as simple in all their appointments and circumstances as were those which made Edward Winslow and Susanna White one; and this, notwithstanding that the dramatic incidents told in the hexameters of Longfellow are probably every one of them purely imaginary, and several of them decidedly anachronistic. Nevertheless, a majority of first readers of "The Courtship of Miles Standish," and many editors and orators, accept this poem as genuine history. In Longfellow's metrical romance, the soldier-widower sends "John Alden, the fair-haired taciturn stripling," as his agent to win Priscilla Mullins' love; but the doughty captain is not the one desired of the maiden, and she hints to the gallant envoy to speak for himself, which, of course, he does. The wedding takes place; but when the service is ended, the sombre, powerful, and armor-clad figure strides in, grasps the bridegroom's hand, and asks forgiveness. Applying the proverb, "No man can gather cherries in Kent at the season of Christmas," he implies that no graybeard can equal a handsome youth in pleading for the hand and heart of a maiden still in life's springtime. Taking each other for husband and wife in the magistrate's presence, "after the Puritan way and the laudable custom of Holland," the bridegroom and the bride go forth and stand at the doorway, while the friends scatter for the labors of the day. Then, from a stall near at hand, amid exclamations of wonder, Alden brings out his "snow-white bull" covered with crimson cloth, and led by a cord that was tied to an iron ring in his muzzle. A cushion is placed for a saddle, that she may ride like a queen on a palfrey, and not tread along like a peasant. Bride and groom move to their new habitation, crossing the ford in the forest. As one pair

> "in the endless succession of lovers,
> So through the Plymouth woods passed onward the bridal procession."

The pictures of John Alden and Priscilla Mullins at their courting show a style of house and furniture probably never seen in old Plymouth colony.

As a simple matter of fact, there were no cattle in the colony at this time, and in a little hamlet with one short street and houses close together, the bridal tour or procession could not have been very long in time or far in space. Nevertheless, we doubt not that the young couple were as happy as if they had been married in a great cathedral with the light streaming in through stained glass, and even with the wedding procession, as in our day, fashionably slow and solemn.

The whole life of the English Separatists was like that set forth in the wonderful pilgrim psalms in that oldest hymn-book of the Church of God, which is written in Hebrew. Theirs was ever "a Song of Ascents." Like good Christians, who knew by sweet experience every one of the blessings named in the Fifth Book of the Psalms, from Number CXX to CXL, each Pilgrim father counted it a great and continual joy to have in his home a "fruitful vine" and plenty of "olive plants" around his table. He rejoiced to have his quiver full. John Alden and his Priscilla were especially permitted to enter into the joys of the 127th and 128th Psalms. The bride's father and mother, with their son, a young man, had died in the first winter's sickness.

Instead of her father, God gave her sons, who with their descendants became as princes in the earth, and her name will be remembered in all generations.

John and Priscilla Alden had eleven children, and were both living in 1650, by which time Priscilla was a grandmother, her oldest daughter having a husband and five children. To-day the descendants of John Alden are like the stars of the heavens in multitude.

As the first marriage was between Edward Winslow and Mrs. White, it is probable that John Alden with Priscilla Mullins made the second, Francis Eaton with Mrs. Carver's servant-maid the third, Bradford with Mrs. Alice Southworth the fourth, and Standish with a lady named Barbara, whose family name is not known, the fifth, John Howland with Elizabeth Tilley the sixth, and Peter Brown with Mrs. Ford the seventh.

No divorces are heard of at Plymouth until forty-one years had passed away, when one woman, on scriptural grounds, obtained a divorce from her husband, who, after being publicly whipped, left the colony. After this, only six cases of divorce are known during the colony's existence, from 1620 to 1691.

There are in the records cases of suits of breach of promise, with the amount of claim and recovery stated. There are instances of men making complaint that their desires of marriage with daughters are frustrated by parents. Several times, the court, after hearing, punished men by threat of fine or whipping for urging unwilling damsels to receive their attentions. In one case the tolerant spirit of John Howland towards the Quakers had angered Governor Thomas Prence, who in 1660 brought suit against Howland's nephew for making love to his daughter without her father's permission. Nevertheless, for seven years, the young couple remained constant to each other. Then the angry father again had the young man brought before the court and fined five pounds, because he had "disorderly and unrighteously" endeavored to obtain the affections of his daughter. So the patient lover was put under a bond of fifty pounds to refrain and desist. Nevertheless, the young man and woman were, a few months later, united in marriage.

Greatly to the delight of those who called the

Pilgrims "Brownists," and who desired and expected that the freedom of the Plymouth Colony would run into anarchy, in order to have the petty prophet's rapture of saying "I told you so," there was much trouble about marriage, after the death of the leaders of the "old stock," on account of radical notions. The second generation, not having won, but only inherited their liberty, went further than the Dutch, who, after instituting civil marriage, safeguarded it most scrupulously. The Plymouth uprooters went so far as to marry themselves, or to get persons without authority to perform the wedding ceremony. In 1654 one man was fined five pounds for disorderly marriage, and then fined five pounds again; and notified that he would be fined every three months, until he came to be married by a magistrate. Later on, three others were mulcted for the same offense.

Perhaps the severity of the Plymouth rulers defeated the very end which they had in view, of maintaining personal purity throughout the whole colony. It does not necessarily follow that the morality of the time or place was below the average in America or England to-day, for no such diligence of search and observation is now known, as was then and there in vogue, nor is the machinery of the law so perfect for the discovery of wrong-doing in social matters. Indeed, considering the abundance and minuteness of the writings concerning the Plymouth men and women and the consequent publicity for all time, their record of general morality is a noble one.

Some of the court proceedings show that both men and women used their tongues in a lively sort of way, calling each other vile names very freely. The magistrates, believing that the tongue being a world of iniquity was sometimes set on fire of Gehenna, punished misuse of this member very severely. When men, by living a vagrant life in the woods, did not treat or support their wives properly, — a disorder very common on the frontier, and one from which the French settlements in Canada suffered mortally, — they were heavily fined. Masters for not instructing their apprentices properly, and any persons for telling lies, were also punished by fines. One man who averred that he had seen a whale when none else had, was fined twenty shillings. Evidently the sea serpent that swims in the newspapers had not then been invented, though even then, on most European maps, all sorts of mythical monsters disported themselves. Another man who told a fib, the size or quality of which is not stated, was fined ten shillings; but the wife of another named George who lied not perniciously, but only "unadvisedly," was discharged.

The records seem to show that at Plymouth, as elsewhere, men not unfrequently tried to make public justice an instrument of private revenge.

We find a number of cases of fines for card-playing; but although there were laws against "the devil's picture-books," with the penalty of corporal punishments, yet we do not learn that they were executed. No doubt a good deal of idle play with colored pasteboard was had privately, in barns and garrets, during which probably very little gambling was done. Stolen water was sweet and bread eaten in secret pleasant then, as in pre-ancient and modern times. A prohibition and "thou shalt not" are always challenges. A positive command to do something good is always the best way of making the Everlasting Kingdom come, and the founders of Plymouth knew and believed in Christ's way. It is not so certain that their immediate successors did, at least in equal measure.

Society in New Plymouth in 1665 was less under the dominion of enlightened Christian gentlemen than it had been in 1625, and was more under the control of a clerical caste. In a word, Plymouth Christianity was then more like that in a state church, and under the politics of paternalism. After 1650 we find several cases of men fined and set in the stocks for staying away from worship and preaching, or for not speaking with sufficient respect of the preachers, who probably were both scholastic and prosy. Dr. Matthew Fuller opposed the new law which laid a compulsory tax for the support of the clergy. For this he was fined fifty shillings. Christians who were Christ-like in their conduct toward the Friends were prosecuted before the courts and fined by those who were bitter against the "Quakers," — the charge being that they were absent from church when they ought to have been there. When sickness and poor crops troubled the superstitious, they held a fast to avert "the Lord's wrath" as shown in his not having made more effectual their brutal and devilish treatment of the Quakers; all of which seems wonderfully like the Israelitish worship of Jehovah through Moloch. Other persons were arrested for not paying the clergy tax. Men were whipped for reviling the parson. In the suits which ministers brought against free-speaking people they were very apt to win their case. All this helped to bring Bradford's gray hairs in sorrow to the grave.

The superstitions of the Plymouth men are worth studying. Bradford and the leaders of the Leyden church were for their age, and as men inheriting the relics of Norse or Germanic paganism, remarkably free from gross notions generated from ignorance. Indeed, throughout his life and in his writings, Bradford shows that he was a devout and a scientific man. He did not make his whims or his ignorance pass for religion. He kept his Christianity free from degrading superstition, which is so much and so often associated with piety and so much nourished or winked at by the clergy for the sake of power over the vulgar.

Eleven years in Holland under the training of Robinson, and a decade in a university town, had greatly clarified and purified the minds of the Plymouth leaders from superstition; but many of the second generation in the wilderness were victims to the fear of earthquake, lightning, comets, and signs in the heaven and earth. In this they were just like pagans, uncivilized men, and weak Christians, who suppose that ignorance and fear which it breeds are parts of religion. A comet was usually supposed to portend calamities, like war, smallpox, or the plague. In a great tail of gas, they saw the Almighty's sword of vengeance.

Altogether, the contrast between the comparative freedom from superstition of the Plymouth old comers, who were mostly from Holland, and those of the Puritans, who came directly from England, is remarkable. There was a constant habit among the latter, though not wholly confined to them, of attributing current events to direct supernatural intervention. Often the record of the writer's subjective fancies is comical. For example, Winthrop, who did not like the English prayer-book, tells us that his son in Connecticut had the Greek Testament, the Psalms, and the prayer-book bound in one volume, and this with others was kept in a room where their corn was stored. The mice, neglecting the other books, gnawed entirely through the prayer-book, and left everything else in the volume untouched. What intelligent mice!

CHAPTER XXIII

THE NEW ENGLAND CONFEDERATION

SCARCELY seventeen summers had passed away in New Plymouth before the wise men of the settlement began to feel the need of union with the other colonies.

The quarrels of the Old had been transported to the New World. It was a very uncertain question as to who should possess North America, — French, Spanish, Dutch, or English. The Indian problem was serious. Little help could be looked for from the home-land, with such sovereigns as the Stuarts on the throne. All Great Britain was in commotion on account of the approaching Scottish and civil wars.

The Plymouth men had seen the advantages of union and federal government in their second home. The motto of the Dutch republic, "Eendracht maagt macht" (unity makes strength), was to them a household word. In the Congress of the United States which met at the Hague, the watchword, in sight of all, was "By concord, little things become great." Their life as Pilgrims had also proved the truth of the 133d Psalm. They also knew the perils and the limitations of federal government.

In the annual synod in Boston in 1637, a civil league was proposed. The Plymouth men began six years of discussion with the three other colonies, one in Massachusetts and two in Connecticut. The result was that in 1643 "The New England Confederation" was formed. It included the four colonies, Massachusetts Bay and Plymouth, Hartford and New Haven. Maine, New Hampshire, and Rhode Island were left out, for Plymouth claimed the territory first settled by Roger Williams, and Massachusetts persisted, in spite of the Gorges family, in reckoning Maine and New Hampshire, notwithstanding Mason's claim, as within the limits of her patent.

Two men, church members, delegates from each colony in the confederation, met annually in September, and in each of the colonies in turn. This little legislature of eight had charge of war and peace, Indian affairs, the rendition of criminals and of runaway servants, the making of roads and communications, the assessment of expenses, and the settlement of boundary disputes. In education and religion, the little congress had only advisory power. Each colony was to manage its own local affairs.

In a word, here was the Dutch federal union in miniature. Connecticut, which borrowed so much and so closely from the republic in which its leaders Hooker and Davenport, like the Pilgrims, had for years found refuge, wanted, like the Dutch states and cities, to have a veto power. She even refused at first to join the league unless she could have it; but the victorious Dutch, having humbled giant Spain, seemed to be expanding in New Netherland and pressing on her borders, while civil war, whose issue no man could foretell, had broken out in England. So Connecticut withdrew her opposition, the union was perfected, and the little congress began its sessions. As in the Dutch States-General, a majority or three fourths vote was necessary for action.

In form the confederation lasted half a century, but its real life covered only about twenty years. It suffered from the same diseases which had troubled the Dutch republic. Massachusetts was its Holland, rich, aristocratic, dictatorial, wanting to use power instead of giving advice, too little inclined to union and helpful coöperation, and too much given to assertion of state-right. No federal government can get along well with such a disproportionately powerful state as Holland in a republic, or with such a large colony as Massachusetts in a little colonial confederation. The disturbance of the system is too great. In 1675, of the 43,000 people in the confederation, about one half were in Massachusetts Bay, with 7000 in Plymouth Colony and 14,000 in Connecticut. Holland, both in guilders and in souls, was nearly equal to all the other six Dutch states, and so also Massachusetts, equal in money and numbers to the others, was the controller of the "United Colonies of New England." Within a decade advisory power, in education and religion, had become something very much like authority, and Puritan bigotry was undermining the Christian tolerance, freedom and simplicity of Plymouth.

In joint stock companies the man who has a majority of shares can "control the stock." Plymouth in the New England Confederation found itself in the condition of the cony that had invited the hedgehog "in its burrow." Bradford's fable was once more illustrated.

Even before the end of the first ten years, Massachusetts began to get Hollandish, and seemed unwilling to submit to the authority of the Union. In 1650, Connecticut, by permission of the congress, having levied taxes to support a fort at the mouth of the Connecticut River, Massachusetts, without authority, laid duties on the commerce of the other colonies, the pretext being to pay for the fort in Boston harbor. This unauthorized assertion of state-right or of nullification destroyed the Union. Thereafter it had only a nominal existence.

In 1653, when the English were fighting a commercial war with the Dutch to get the carrying trade of the ocean, Connecticut wanted the colonies to invade New Netherland, and the congress passed a majority vote for war; but Massachusetts, contrary to the Constitution, demanded unanimous consent for offensive action. After 1663 the sessions of the congress became triennial. In 1667 Plymouth Colony made a strong protest against the behavior of the predominant colony and its unjust emphasis laid on its "state-right." Besides wanting the capital, or the sessions of the congress, to be at Boston and its president a Massachusetts man, the largest of the colonies objected to the vital principle of federal government — the equal representation of the colonies. This was the soul of the Dutch republic, and is still the fundamental principle in the Senate of the United States of America.

When the English commonwealth gave way to the Restoration, Charles II. paid little or no attention to the confederation. In 1686 under James II. the congress of the colonies adopted a flag that must have pleased this royal person, if indeed he did not order its design. It was a huge red cross set upright on a white ground, with the king's monogram and crown in gold in the centre. For ships, the flag was red, with a white cross resting on a white union of the crosses of St. Andrew and St. George, in the upper left-hand corner of which was a pine-tree.

The last triennial session of the little federal congress was held in Hartford in 1684. Two years later, Sir Edmund Andros, the tool of that royal law-breaker, James II., blotted out the

Union and trampled on all law. In 1692 Governor Phips arrived. He was armed with authority from the Dutch king, William III., of Great Britain and Ireland. The charter which Phips bore combined Nova Scotia, Maine, the Vineyard Archipelago, and the colonies on Massachusetts Bay into the one British province of Massachusetts. New Plymouth, with her seventeen towns and 13,000 people, ceased to exist, except as a glorious memory and a noble name.

The poetic and heroic era of the Pilgrim story ended with the New England Confederation. "From this period, but not alone from this cause, Plymouth history ceases to be of *continuous* interest."

Of the heroes and leaders, as well as most of the rank and file, it may be written: —

"These all died in faith, not having received the promises, but having seen them and greeted them from afar, and having confessed that they were strangers and pilgrims on the earth."

CHAPTER XXIV

TRANSFIGURATION

THERE are two ways of writing history, even as there is a twofold method of expression. The one follows the analogy taught by the Master, in which the mustard-seed becomes, visibly, a great tree. The other makes real the likeness of the leaven which invisibly transforms. In the second parable, sour dough transmutes flour into bread, sweet and wholesome. The one change is external to the eye, the other is inward to the life, recognizable by the taste, nerves, and spirit.

I prefer to tell of the vitalizing power of principles, which, unseen and potent, transform the lower into the higher forms. The narrative of a movement or people, as constructed only from parchments and papers, seals and documents, is the story of a skeleton, rather than of a living organism. Besides writings and pictures, there are other methods of revealing the sequence of cause and effect and of expressing the reality of results.

Besides books, eulogies, and after-dinner oratory, which transfigure the past, one may show forth the doings of ancestors — whether spiritual or after the flesh — by re-creating their environment. As a judicial critic, and not merely as a local panegyrist, one may rear also on the ancient sites and in the old homes more than one "durable token of appreciation."

Hence, after writing this book on the Pilgrims, the author sought to show, more particularly in Holland, their second home, the Boston Club's "grateful recognition of Dutch hospitality." These English refugees, as William Bradford in his deathless history declared, when persecuted in the British Isles, "by a joint consent . . . resolved to go into the Low Countries where they heard was freedom of religion for all men," and were there aided and welcomed.

There, despite the ungenerous silence of so many writers of American history, these country folks were mightily reinforced in intellect and practical wisdom. The author, in 1890, subscribed to the great bronze tablet erected on the wall of St. Peter's Church in Leyden, in July, 1891, by the National Council of the Congregational Churches of the United States of America, in honor of John Robinson; yet his protest, though silent, was none the less real and deeply felt against the state of mind which could compose and retain an inscription, which reveals no trace of appreciation or gratitude to the Dutch Government, people, municipality, or the University of Leyden, which sheltered the fugitives from the wrath of James Stuart. The text on the tablet which contains also a bas-relief of the historic ship reads:—

THE MAYFLOWER, 1620.

In Memory of

REV. JOHN ROBINSON, M.A.

Pastor of The English Church worshipping over against this spot, A.D. 1609–1625, whence at his prompting went forth

THE PILGRIM FATHERS,

to settle in New England

in 1620.

Buried under this house of worship

4 March, 1625

Aet. XLIX. years

In memoria æterna erit justus.

Erected by the National Council of the Congregational Churches of the United States of America,

AD. 1891.

In the brick façade of the Pesyn Hof, or Home for Aged Walloons (pp. 126–131) is a stone slab on which is inscribed: —

On this spot

lived, taught and died

JOHN ROBINSON, 1611–25

Returning home, in 1891, I started a campaign of interest and a financial movement that secured the erection of memorial tablets in honor of the English Separatists in the Scotch Church at Middelburg (pp. 50–66, 67), and in that of the

Beguynhof, at Amsterdam (p. 73), and in the Reformed Church at Delfshaven (p. 164). The inscriptions, and especially the emblematic decorations, witnesses centuries old, express eloquently both facts and feelings. With appropriate ceremonies, of historical reminiscence, dedication and reception by the proper authorities, these bronze tablets were unveiled in the years, 1906, 1909, and 1913, respectively.

Whether they would or not, the Pilgrims were called "Brownists," after Robert Browne (pp. 50, 66, 67). As each tablet speaks for itself, we give herewith in the chronological order of history, and not of affixing, the text of each, noting also the symbolic embellishments which are themselves eloquent.

On the first are the arms of the two countries —the eagle and stars of the United States of America and the lion and the motto of the Netherlands, the Indian of Massachusetts and the swimming lion of Zealand, the seals of the city of Middelburg, of the National Congregational Sunday School and Publishing Society, and of the Reformed Church in America, which latter emblem contains the heraldry of William of Nassau, called posthumously "the Silent."

1582 1913
ONE IN CHRIST
TO THE GLORY OF THE TRIUNE GOD
IN HONOR OF WILLIAM OF NASSAU AND THE HOSPITABLE
CITY OF MIDDELBURG AND TO THE FOUNDERS OF
MODERN CONGREGATIONAL ORDER
BROWNE · CARTWRIGHT · HARRISON
THE CONGREGATIONAL SUNDAY SCHOOLS OF THE
UNITED STATES OF AMERICA
GRATEFULLY REAR THIS MEMORIAL
SEPTEMBER 1913

On the second tablet, in the English church in the Beguynhof in Amsterdam, one reads: —

ONE IN CHRIST
1609 — FROM SCROOBY TO AMSTERDAM — 1909
AINSWORTH · JOHNSON · ROBINSON · BREWSTER · BRADFORD
"BY A JOINT CONSENT THEY RESOLVED TO GO INTO THE LOW COUNTRIES
WHERE THEY HEARD WAS FREEDOM OF RELIGION FOR ALL MEN
AND LIVED AT AMSTERDAM"
(GOVERNOR WILLIAM BRADFORD: HISTORY OF PLYMOUTH PLANTATION)
IN GRATEFUL REMEMBRANCE AND IN CHRISTIAN BROTHERHOOD
THE CHICAGO CONGREGATIONAL CLUB
REARS THIS MEMORIAL
A.D. 1909

Beside the lettering, one discerns on this tablet the arms of the State of Illinois and of the cities of Chicago and Amsterdam, the lion of the Netherlands and the seal of the Amsterdam church and of the Chicago Congregational Club; which latter bears the effigy of the Mayflower sailing into Lake Michigan and making hail in front of Fort Dearborn, the nucleus, in 1804, and on the frontier, of the giant city of to-day.

This Amsterdam Memorial has developed a magnetic power and influence only slightly anticipated by the donors. Besides attracting English-speaking tourists on the week-days, it has doubled the attendance on the Sabbath of American and British worshipers.

In Amsterdam, renowned in the annals of freedom of conscience, of Anglo-Dutch and American-Hollandish scholarship and hymnology, and of ecclesiastical, political, and commercial relations, there is a street named after the English refugees in this city on the Y.

At Delfshaven now, with the Ruige Platt (p. 165), a part of the city of Rotterdam, there is, in the Consistory Room of the church edifice, the engraving of Schwartzé's painting of the scene in 1621, in the Common House (p. 200), at Plymouth. In the north wall is set a stone from Chicago, inscribed in Greek with the monogram of the Christ, presented by the late E. W. Blatchford, long a deacon of the New England Congregational Church in Chicago, in the façade of which he set a slab from each of the Pilgrims' three homes — Scrooby, Delfshaven, and Plymouth Rock. In the great fire in Chicago, of October 8, 1871, which gutted the sacred edifice, the three memorial stones were left, like the three children in the fiery furnace, scathless by the flames. The south wall of the Delfshaven church bears in letters of enduring bronze the tablet inscription, an ample token of the gratitude of the living Pilgrims, in words penned by Bradford in 1627:—

ONE IN CHRIST
FROM DELFSHAVEN JULY 22 A.D. 1620
THE PILGRIM FATHERS BEGAN THEIR VOYAGE TO NEW ENGLAND

"OBLIGED BY THE GOOD AND COURTEOUS ENTREATY
WHICH WE HAVE FOUND IN YOUR COUNTRY
WE AND OUR CHILDREN ARE BOUND TO BE THANKFUL"
(GOVERNOR WILLIAM BRADFORD TO THE DUTCH ON MANHATTAN MARCH 19 1627)
IN TOKEN OF ENDURING GRATITUDE AND IN CHRISTIAN BROTHERHOOD
THE BOSTON CONGREGATIONAL CLUB REARS THIS MEMORIAL
JULY 1906

The symbols in the upper portion show the seal of Massachusetts, of the church at Delfshaven, and of the former port of Delft, now incorporated in Rotterdam.

When on Friday evening, September 28, 1906, the author, at the tablet-unveiling exercises, delivered the historical address, there sat prominently in the front of the crowded auditorium about a dozen young men. At every patriotic allusion to things American, they showed visible or audible signs of interest, sometimes approaching to rapture. The formal exercises over, the auditors met socially in the Consistory Room and inscribed their names. Supposing these young men to be a party of American students, the author asked one, who seemed to be the leader, whether he and his companions were from Harvard or Cornell. The answer was, "No, we are Mormon missionaries!!"

Tourists will find in the ancient edifice at Delfshaven, on the table, the record book for visitors and on the wall a framed engraving of the great painting by Johan Georg Schwartzé, father of Teresa Schwartzé-van Duyl, long the greatest of living woman painters. The model for the little girl standing by the cradle was the painter's daughter, whose pictures of orphan girls, in tile and on canvas, are now famous in many lands. The original oil painting, representing many years of work, both of research and with palette and easel, was sent to America for exhibition, but the ship carrying it was sunk by the guns of the Confederate cruiser Alabama. Happily fifty copies of a reduced lithograph of the painting were struck off. Dying of his disappointment, the father-painter predicted the greatness of his artist daughter.

Ten bronze tablets erected in the Netherlands by the author, besides three others (two at Leyden and one at Zwolle) by societies, to commemorate events, persons, or points of contact between American and Dutch history, make the Netherlands, the second home of the Pilgrims, to their descendants both interesting and cultural; especially as American historians have, for the most part, ignored both the Dutch influences in the making of the United States and the principles and institutions which the Pilgrims and Puritans and our Revolutionary and Constitutional fathers borrowed so freely and consciously from the Republic of the United Netherlands.

England, first home of these sons of light and freedom, is also waking up and taking pride in her children who, after reinforcement in a federal republic, crossed the sea and, in the wilderness, transplanted the best ideas of the Briton, the Netherlander, and the Continental, expressing them in social structures and political institutions. The majority of the passengers in the Pilgrim ships to America — the Speedwell, Mayflower, Fortune, Little James, and Anne, as well as those of the Charity and Swan (p. 222) — were of English birth or descent. Yet there were in the Pilgrim company no fewer than seven nationalities represented, — English, Scotch, Irish, Welsh, Dutch, Walloon and German, besides several varieties of religion. In spirit the individuals of this cosmopolitan company were in reality as remote from the imaginary and idealized persons of certain after-dinner orators as they were radically different from the Puritans. Their homesickness and exile, hardships and vicissitudes, had so tempered them that, in America, they could fraternize with John Alden, who was most probably an Irishman, one of the Irish Aldens; with Miles Standish, who was never a member of the Pilgrim Church and was most probably, certainly until very late in life, a Catholic; and with Roger Williams the radical, who was expelled by the Puritans, not because of theological, but rather of political heresies; for he believed both in William the Silent's ideas of toleration and that the Indians were the real owners of the soil.

The legislation of the Pilgrims proved their broadmindedness and belief in the principles of the federal republic, in which they had lived so long and learned so much.

Nevertheless, even a President of the United States, in his oration at the laying of the cornerstone at Provincetown, August 20, 1907, never so much as used the word "Pilgrim," and talked about Puritans. In Philadelphia there stood for years, in front of the City Hall, the well-known bronze statue by St. Gaudens of Elder Pynchon, of Springfield, who was a stern Puritan. Underneath, on the pedestal, was cut the inscription "The Pilgrim." The after-dinner speaking at New England Societies still shows traces of this unjust confusion of thought.

In England, the unadorned inscription on the tablet placed upon the Scrooby manor house may be read as follows:—

THIS TABLET IS ERECTED BY THE
PILGRIM SOCIETY OF PLYMOUTH
MASSACHUSETTS, UNITED STATES OF
AMERICA, TO MARK THE SITE OF THE
ANCIENT MANOR HOUSE, WHERE LIVED
WILLIAM BREWSTER
FROM 1588 TO 1608, AND WHERE HE
ORGANIZED THE PILGRIM CHURCH, OF
WHICH HE BECAME RULING ELDER, AND
WITH WHICH IN 1608, HE REMOVED TO
AMSTERDAM, IN 1609 TO LEYDEN, AND IN
1620 TO PLYMOUTH, WHERE HE DIED
APRIL 16 1644.

In Plymouth, England, after the visit thither of the delegates to the International Congregational Council, held in London, in July, 1891, there were placed in the City Hall memorial windows and on the Barbican a granite slab containing a bronze tablet in honor of the Pilgrims. At Southampton, England, August 15, 1913, on the 293d anniversary of the sailing of the Mayflower, there was unveiled, in honor of the Pilgrims, by the citizens and the friends of Hartley University College, an artistic shaft of rough hewn Portland stone, fifty feet high, and surmounted by an Ionic cupola carried upon eight slender columns against a mosaic of white and gold. Topping the cupola itself is a ship under full sail, forged in copper and representing the Mayflower.

At Gainsborough, the cornerstone of the John Robinson Memorial Church, in honor of the noble, self-effacing pastor of the Pilgrims, was laid June 9, 1906. In the completed edifice, in 1909, the author had the pleasure of lecturing on "The Pilgrims in Their Three Homes."

In a number of the English Congregational church edifices, one may now see numerous memorials in stained glass representing scenes and characters in the Pilgrim movement. In America, as æsthetic taste dominates more in ecclesiastical architecture, once so plain, this form of commemoration has become quite general.

All other Pilgrim movements, however, were thrown into the shade by the completion, at Provincetown, Massachusetts, of the lofty and graceful tower (which follows the model of that at Siena, Italy) which was dedicated with imposing exercises on August 5, 1910. Besides being 210 feet high from the base, it serves as a beacon and landmark to men at sea. It replaced a bronze tablet erected by the Commonwealth of Massachusetts to commemorate the signing of the Mayflower Covenant (p. 183). President Taft of the United States and Charles W. Eliot of Harvard University delivered addresses. The following hymn, composed by the author of this book, and set to music by Lester M. Bartlett, was sung by a quartette from Boston, both at the dedication exercises and also at their banquet, as it had been sung also at the laying of the corner-stone four years before.

The text of this hymn, with number, tune, metre, name, and footnote, is reprinted from "The Pilgrim Hymnal," Boston, 1909.

421

Duke Street

L. M.

1 Forth from their mother-land outcast,
  Our fathers fled to find a home;
Long dwelt they guests, in conscience free,
  Within a State without a throne.

2 Thou wast their King, their Judge, their Law,
  Their Guiding Star across the deep,
Here on this strand they bent the knee,
  And vowed thy covenant to keep.

3 They reared a beacon for our faith,
  And we would follow them, as they
Marched with the Captain of their souls,
  Our service sweet in freedom's way.

4 Spirit of truth, lead us their sons,
  Let light e'er break forth from thy Word,
Our hearts incline, with grace inspire
  Our souls to dare and do, O Lord!

WILLIAM ELLIOT GRIFFIS, D.D., L.H.D.

Sung August 20, 1907, at the laying of the corner-stone of the Memorial of the first landing of the Pilgrim Fathers of New England at Provincetown, Mass., November 21, 1620.

The full story of the Provincetown Memorial is told in the volume by Dr. E. J. Carpenter, entitled "The Pilgrims and Their Monument," New York, 1911.

Notable memorials in art are the mural painting of Mr. Henry Oliver Walker in the Massachusetts State House, representing the men on the deck of the Mayflower when they caught sight of the land in America (p. 179); and a picture of the historic vessel by Mr. Marshall Johnson, which some think should replace the Indian, the mailed arm and the sword and the rather militant motto on the old seal of Massachusetts.

In Central Park, New York, stands the bronze statue of "The Pilgrim," of heroic size, the artistic work of the great sculptor, John Quincy Adams Ward. No suggestion of senility, or of scholastic, ecclesiastical, or theological import is here. It is the effigy of a stalwart man, in the prime of health and vigor, clad in the costume of his day, his gun in hand, and bandoliers across his jerkin — a true and inspiring conception. The four bas-reliefs in granite, on the façade of the Congregational House, No. 14 Beacon Street, Boston — itself a noble memorial in architecture to the Pilgrims — were wrought by a Spanish sculptor in 1898. Two of them tell of initial Pilgrim experiences in America, the Mayflower cabin and on Clarke's Island, and two refer to the Puritans. One represents John Eliot preaching to the Indians and the other tells of the founding of Harvard College — on whose roll only two names of students from the Pilgrim or Old Colony, and only two graduates living at Plymouth before 1690, are found.

In literature, the sumptuous annotated edition of Bradford's "History of Plymouth Plantation," issued by the Massachusetts Historical Society in 1913; "The Log of the Mayflower," by Azel Ames; "The England and Holland of the Pilgrims," by Rev. Morton Dexter; "The Pilgrims," by Dr. F. A. Noble; "The Pilgrim Faith," by Dr. Ozora Davis; "The Romantic Story of the Mayflower Pilgrims," by Albert C. Addison, and other monographs issued since 1898, show how rich is the mine, whose central lode, the Pilgrim Life in Holland, is not yet fully explored. In 1904 the "General Society of Mayflower Descendants" was formed which published several volumes of "The Mayflower Descendant." The social club called "The Pilgrims," organized in 1902 in London, to promote good fellowship and friendliness between the American and British nations, and made up of English-speaking people on both sides of the Atlantic has now a thousand members. In 1914, the centennial also of the birth of John Lothrop Motley, the Anglo-American Exposition, from May to October, at Shepherd's Bush in London, commemorates the century of peace between the two nations.

The ter-centenary of the landing upon Plymouth Rock is, at this writing, not far distant. Its celebration on both sides of the Atlantic should strengthen the chain binding together the English-speaking nations.

INDEX

INDEX TO CHAPTER XXIV